NEWPORT: A Writer's Beginnings

Mary C. Connolly

from

Kathy Byron Kahr

The chapter entitled "The Colonel" first appeared in *Sin Fronteras*, Winter, 2006. It was subsequently anthologized in *One Hundred Great Essays*, edited by Robert DiYanni (Penguin Academics Series, Third Edition). New York/London, 2008.

The chapter entitled "Diamonds Are Forever" was first presented as a multi-media performance at the *Images in Motion Baseball Exhibition* at the Oakland Museum of California. Copyright © 1988 by Michael Hogan.

Cover Photo credit: 15 September 1962 President Kennedy waves to the America's Cup crew of the "Weatherly". Aboard the USS Joseph P. Kennedy, Jr., off Newport, Rhode Island. Photograph by Cecil Stoughton, White House, in the John F. Kennedy Presidential Library and Museum, Boston.

NEWPORT

A Writer's Beginnings

MICHAEL HOGAN

Thus freedom always came nibbling at my thought,
just as—often, in light, on the open hills—
you can pass an antelope and not know
and look back and then—even before you see—
there is something wrong about the grass.
And then you see.

That's the way everything in the world is waiting.

—from "A Message from the Wanderer" by William Stafford

CHAPTERS

THIRD SUNDAY AFTER PENTECOST

And there's nothing short of dying
half as lonely as the sound
of a Sunday morning sidewalk
and Sunday morning coming down.
                    --Kris Kristofferson

SUNDAY. HOW THE HOURS weigh us down, like a double quilt on a bed when the night suddenly turns warm and we awake, suffocating. How the minutes hang heavy like those at an airport as we wait for a flight that's been delayed by weather.

Any Sunday is bad enough, but the worst is a rainy Sunday when the ingrained inertia of the day is doubled and drops of rain on the roof reverberate like the seconds of a clock ticking backwards. Hemingway, in his *Farewell to Arms*, has a young lieutenant in a military hospital looking at the rain and seeing himself dead out there. We don't know if it's a Sunday in the novel, but it probably is. Any other day of the week he'd be too busy with shots, and nurses drawing blood, with visitors and noise on the ward to harbor such thoughts. Thomas DeQuincy, that old addict, wrote: "There is no duller spectacle on this earth of ours than a rainy Sunday in London."

In my drinking days it was worse. To awake on a Sunday morning in Denver hung-over and shaky and know that there were no bars, no liquor stores open, because of antiquated "blue laws" passed by teetotalers a

1

century before was bad enough. But there was also the blinding headache, the futile fumbling through ashtrays for a leftover roach; the frantic search through the house for the last half-inch remaining in the bottles from Saturday night's revels. Then, the drinking of ice water, the dry heaves, followed by a return to bed: chilled, antsy, unable to get back to sleep, followed by promises to quit forever, and the useless, unanswered (perhaps because insincere) prayers.

Speaking of prayer. What used to give substance to Sundays in our childhood back in the Fifties was attendance at church. We may not have liked it much but at least there was some structure to part of the day. We woke early, washed up, dressed in our Sunday finest and walked to the church with Mom, Dad and Sister. The liturgy was clearly defined. It not only gave shape to the day but provided a pattern for the year. It was, for example, Palm Sunday with its welcome story of Jesus' entry into the city. Then after Mass, the gift of the blessed palm fronds in the vestibule, and the fashioning of them into little crosses at home, with the expectation of Easter on the horizon. Or it was the second Sunday in Advent, or the Third Sunday in Pentecost, Septuagesima Sunday, Candlemas Sunday, each with its own colors, its own Biblical story, prayers and hymns. Now, we don't even remember what half those terms meant. Sundays have no shape at all.

In the days of my youth, Catholic boys and girls went to Mass, returned home to a rich and leisurely breakfast of pancakes, scrambled eggs and bacon. It was a ceremonial breakfast as opposed to the usual fare of oatmeal and toast served most weekday mornings. Then the fat Sunday papers with the colored comics for the kids, weekly sports summaries for Grandpa, in-depth news analysis for Dad, and fashions and recipes for Mom. Then a walk to the park while the Sunday roast slowly simmered and filled the house with rich odors, and we waved to the neighbors sitting on their porches, and crossed the streets without looking both ways because there was so little traffic you could hear the occasional car coming long before it reached your block.

Our appetites sharpened by the walk, we returned home to the pork roast, or roast beef, the French beans, the rich gravy and mashed potatoes, the biscuits hot from the oven which we'd slice open and fill with butter so that they dripped as we lifted them to our mouths.

When Sunday dinner was done and the dishes washed, Mother would undo her apron and comb her hair. Dad and I would go out to the driveway and take a chamois cloth to the car to wipe away any smudge on the Simonized surface. Then we'd all pile into the station wagon for a Sunday drive around town and then out to the countryside. We'd count the number of sheep or cows in a field, the out-of-state license plates of the cars we passed (never more than two or three), and play word games, sing songs, or recite verses we'd learned at school. There was a car radio, but it was seldom played on Sunday. Dad would have liked to listen to the Red Sox game, Mom to Patti Paige, we kids to Elvis or Jerry Lee Lewis. But since we could not all have it our own way, none of us did.

Then ice cream on the return home and the long winding down of the afternoon as we each retreated into our private corners of the house: Dad to hear the re-cap of the ballgame and ultimately to fall asleep in his armchair snoring gently; Mom to catch up on her sewing or to read a neglected novel; my sister and I to do homework assignments or play records (quietly because it's Sunday). Then a light supper after which we'd gather around to hear Bishop Fulton J. Sheen castigate the Communists on "Life Is Worth Living" and then the Ed Sullivan Show with its odd mixture of family comedy, dull Hit Parade music, circus acts and surprises like Elvis and the Beatles. As I tell my Mexican students, it was the *Sabado Gigante* for Sunday in Fifties "Gringolandia." (For those who don't watch Spanish TV, there simply exists no other point of comparison.) After Ed Sullivan, we each retreated to our rooms where we got our clothes ready for Monday school or work, bathed and brushed our teeth, then curled up with a book or magazine until we fell asleep.

Sundays had a clear shape to them then, although the outlines were fuzzy and some were better than others. There were Sunday mornings when the sermon was boring or the hymns off-key; when someone was wearing the same new outfit as my mother; or when my sister was snubbed by a group of girls with whom she had been fast friends only days before. There were afternoons when the smoke from Dad's cigarette and an undigested piece of beef would produce car sickness on the Sunday drive in one or both of us kids. There were evenings when the TV was on the fritz, or when there was "nothing at all to read," or when the house was heavy with the silences of my parents' anger. Still, Sundays were ritualistic and family-centered, comforting in their sameness, dependable, habitual. And if we sometimes felt that there was a lack of freedom to do our own thing, to be alone, to think deep thoughts, there were—in retrospect—islands of self-awareness and peace. We were left on our own at church to think our own thoughts; we could converse or ramble along silently on our morning walks. After the Sunday drive we could retreat to our rooms to read, to write in our journals, or simply lie on the bed and stare at the ceiling. And at night we could retire early to review our day and plan the week ahead.

As we got older and went out into the world to cobble together our own shapeless Sundays, the disciplines of family and religion gradually fell away due to distance, independence, jobs abroad, new cultures and new people. In most places there is still the *Sunday Times*, but now it is mostly page after page of advertising, trying like all of corporate America (and its globalized partners) not to entertain or enlighten us, but to convince us that we are incomplete and can never be whole without the latest in perfume, jewelry, health care products, automobiles and cruises to Alaska or the Caribbean.

Church is still an option for some Pentecostal folks who shout and sing and then listen to an entertaining preacher. But the Catholics have kind of lost it. They've surrendered the beauty and mystery of Latin Mass, Gregorian music and sonorous hymns, for a contemporary post-Vatican II tepidness composed of insipid language, watered-down homilies and unsingable hymns. The only relief from this banality is the announcements of fund-raising projects and the list of sick and dying parishioners to remember in our prayers.

There's still the late breakfast but, even if we sleep in and don't eat until noon, we are still left with half the day. The afternoon hangs heavy as the storm clouds that now threaten outside the window of my study as I write this on a gloomy Sunday afternoon.

There are, I suppose, a few places left where a Sunday afternoon drive is still enjoyable. Perhaps the Ocean Drive in Newport, cruising past the Breakers on the cold Atlantic in the dead of winter, or the Rambla along the Rio Plata circling Montevideo. But in most places the traffic is too ugly and congested and driving is not much fun. It is something you must do on a weekday commute to work; not a pleasant pastime for a Sunday afternoon. So we clean out the closets, iron clothes for Monday, page indifferently through magazines, and wait for someone to call. In the evening we listlessly watch inane programming on TV, or try to feign an interest in a minimalist novel as short on plot as it is on substance.

More suicides are committed on Sunday afternoons than at any other time. Even more distressing, more teen suicides occur between the hours of 1 PM and 10 PM on Sunday.

Not hemmed in by old religions, dead languages, worn-out rituals and the demands of family, we are free to do whatever we wish on Sundays. In *Middlemarch*, "poor Dagly read a few verses on a Sunday evening, and the world was at least not darker than it had been before." But for many of us filling the hole that is Sunday is not so easy, and judging by the suicide statistics, the number of those who find the world much darker, unlike "poor Dagly," grows each year.

Unable to accept the hypocrisy which goes with most church attendance, even those who are nominally Christian often opt to stay at home on a Sunday. As preachers voice their support of the war with Iraq or

Afghanistan, embrace the death penalty but deplore abortion as murder, and sing the praises of Israel's slaughter of Lebanese civilians because it hastens the Apocalypse and the return of Christ, staying home seems a sensible choice. For Jews, Buddhists, Hindus and millions of others, Sunday has never been a day that was particularly holy or special. It may be that they are exempt from the statistics which I noted earlier. But I doubt it. Setting the day aside has become an existential black hole, transcending culture and religion. We are all stuck with our Sunday afternoon of the soul.

Maybe the Catholics have at least part of it right with their half-empty churches of ageing parishioners listening to the priest drone on with his announcements of the sick and the dying who need our prayers. "Ask not for whom the bell tolls;" we are all sick and dying. Only what moves us has meaning. And the irony is that by taking away the rituals which shaped our Sundays, we are left with a spiritual vacuum which we are now free to fill as we wish, but often lack the inner resources or will to do so. William James a century ago warned of dropping habits and rituals unless they were replaced by others more salubrious. "The hell to be endured hereafter after of which theology tells," he wrote, "is nothing compared with the hell we make for ourselves in this world." Free of the demands of school and work, of appointments and dead-lines, we get to live with ourselves for a bit on a Sunday afternoon, and many of us discover to our distress how poorly furnished our souls are for the task.

Join with me now as we return to a time when the world appeared to move a bit slower and more deliberately on its wobbly axis. Although life was no less brutal and relationships no less complex, there was still the sense (at least in our small town) that the spiritual played a role in the lives of those around us and that we were part of continuum that reached back a millennium and forward into eternity.

MAME, DOUGHBOYS, WORDS AND A.M.D.G.

I'LL WORK BACKWARDS BECAUSE I know how annoying abbreviations can be to a reader. A.M.D.G. stands for *Ad Majorem Dei Gloriam*, "For the Greater Glory of God."

It was what the Jesuits wrote on the blackboard in class above the calculus problems or the list of Aristotle's elements of the tragic hero. Catholic school was like that when I was a youngster. Knowledge and the difficulty of its acquisition were offered up like a cross. Later, as we copied the letters at the top of our compositions or our final exams, they formed a simple prayer of forlorn hope for a passing grade.

These days I see a larger lesson in the Latin letters, especially now as I type them on the page: A.M.D.G. I think that, as T.S. Eliot wrote, we stand on the shoulders of those who have gone before us. Those whose words, whose intellects, whose spirits are the gifts we have inherited. From them we make a different world than theirs but we build our extension bridges from the solid pylons they provided.

As a writer and teacher I've had excellent models for language: John Henry Newman, T.S. Eliot, Dylan Thomas, William Stafford, and Annie Dillard— to name a few— who taught me the textures of words, the delicacy of diction, and the intricacy of sentence weaving. Those are good things to have, as is the simple joy in language which makes teaching such a pleasure.

But language is, as Hamlet said, "Words, words, words...." And, without the embodiment of soul and of purpose, no matter how beautifully words are strung together, they are lifeless as the manikins in a department store window. Each writer who has had the pleasure of seeing his or her work published, a poem, a story, an essay which moved someone else, knows that when words come alive it is a combination of craft and inspiration that is fortuitous and quite beyond the author's modest talents. It has to do with power outside the writer; it has to do with spirit.

For me the gift of spirit came from my grandmother, a woman everyone called Mame when I was a child. She was a Mame or Madame in the Old World sense: buxom, wholesome, with a Victorian propriety which had survived four wars (the Spanish-American, the Great War, and World War II and Korea), and the loss of a son, my uncle, at the Battle of the Bulge.

She knew more than most parents and most Jesuits about values like courage, generosity and smiling stoicism, and could quote chapter and verse if needed. She honored me with a spontaneous, uncritical love which expressed itself in hearty breakfasts of bacon, doughboys (delicious medallions of fried quick bread), buttered scrambled eggs and coffee sweetened with cream from the top of the bottle. She favored me and pampered me as one does with the last of the male line.

One day as I was coming home from my third grade class, some older boys took my Irish tweed cap from off my head and tossed it around like a football. When I tried to get it back, they teased me into tears and then contemptuously threw the hat up into the branches of a large maple tree.

I ran to Mame's house, dried my tears, and then sat down waiting for the vanilla wafers and iced ginger ale which was our after-school ritual. No refreshments appeared. Instead of greeting me with her usual warmth, Mame was sitting quietly by a window seat from which she had obviously witnessed my humiliation.

"Where are the cookies, Grandma?" I asked.

She looked up at me with no hint of a twinkle in her blue eyes. "Where is your tweed cap?" she asked.

"Some boys took it," I said. "Big boys," I added, so that she would not think me too much of a coward.

"Then you'll just have to get it back," she answered. And there was a hardness in her voice that I had never guessed possible.

"Will you go with me, Grandma?" I asked plaintively.

"No," she said. "That is one thing a grandma can't do for a boy. You must get it yourself, and you must do it for me because I can't afford to buy you another."

"But what will I say to them?" I whined.

She turned to me with a fierce Irish face and, with a voice I never could have imagined, spat out: "You get that damn cap out of the tree NOW!"

I went back to the school yard and, without a second's hesitation, went up to the biggest of the boys and ordered: "You get that damn cap out of the tree NOW!"

The boy, too shocked by my bold tone or too cowardly, climbed up the tree branch and tossed down the cap. The others looked idly on.

I marched back to Mame's house, my pride of accomplishment tinged slightly with wonder. I sat down to my usual treat of vanilla wafers and ginger ale. Nothing more was ever said and the incident was never repeated.

The words she gave me, the inflection, the tough snarl that I imitated, worked. They empowered me in a way which seemed magical then. But I understand now that the spiritual force behind those words was love, and the fear of loss that the tweed cap represented. Something given in love, I learned, is irreplaceable and thus must be fiercely cherished.

When Mame died I was the altar boy at the high requiem mass and I followed the priest around her bronze-handled coffin with the thurible in a cloud of incense intoning the words of the *Dies Irae* in Latin: "The day of wrath when the heavens and the earth shall be moved and the Lord will come to judge the world...." The tears streamed down my face and I was inconsolable. My grandfather even more so. He died himself three months later from a heart which, though previously sound, suddenly stopped as if broken.

Each time I sit down to write, each time I walk into a classroom, Mame is with me: the uncritical love in her eyes, the clear inflection, and the willingness to make unequivocal challenges to the child she loved. Thinking of her, I know that all of our gifts, whether they are Irish caps, or language, or a student's grasp of a new idea, are blessed by love and irreplaceable. They are to be cherished, and are always worth speaking up for, fiercely when necessary. And not out of arrogance or pride, but *ad majorem Dei gloriam*, this one life, those school days, and words spoken truly and from the heart.

SWIMMING

IT WAS NOT YET summer in the coastal New England town. The June breeze still had the chill of March in it; yet classes were over for the school year, and I had gone with the public school boys out to the piers at King's Park. I was nine years old and while attending St. Augustine's School usually played with my contemporaries and classmates. But once summer arrived, I tagged along with the tougher kids from the Irish Fifth Ward who went to public schools. The Gashouse Gang, as they would become known to the neighborhood and the police in the years to come, played games that always seemed to me more exciting than those of my school friends. Yet, they were also more dangerous.

There was the time, for example, they stole a twelve-meter yacht and sailed it far out beyond Breton's point where it capsized and could have drowned the lot of them if a Coast Guard cutter had not been in the vicinity. Another time, swimming in the forbidden channel of Narragansett Bay, they chanced upon an orange float. They pulled it behind them, thinking to take it to a cove to use later as a raft (a la Huck Finn) when a Navy chopper came rattling out of the heavens spewing machine-gun fire and sank it. It almost killed them in the process. The shiny orange float, you see, was a target used for aerial gunnery practice.

13

They were older and tougher than I. Most of them were in junior high; two were in high school. They let me hang out with them because my Uncle Harry was a famous war hero. Out Little League field had been named after him and I was able to tell them stories of World War II which (though often exaggerated and sometimes made out of whole cloth) had the power of authenticity and presence. I had impressive documentation and Uncle Harry could not come back to refute me by telling his own story. There were his letters home, the field reports, the official message of condolence from President Roosevelt to my grandmother after his death, the note from his commanding officer, the citation which came with his final medal and his corpse. He had fought at the Battle of the Bulge and received any number of combat decorations which I occasionally snuck out of the house, along with a canteen, a bayonet, and some of my father's Old Gold or Camel cigarettes.

The Gashouse Gang thus tolerated me despite my youth. Also, like any adolescent gang, they liked the opportunity of having a novice to teach, a scapegoat to blame, and a little kid to trick when they were bored. I was actually a kind of mascot and most of the time they were protective of me. But not always.

This particular day in June was chilly, as I said. But the gang leader, Eddie Fitzgerald also known as Fitz, said, "Let's go swimming off the pier." Everybody agreed enthusiastically, and headed out the long municipal pier. There was a cool breeze blowing and the water around the pilings was choppy. Milk-colored foam hung to the sides. There were also pools of oil gleaming phosphorescently. There were plastic cups in the cold dark water and used

14

condoms. It was, to say the least, not an attractive place to go swimming. But going to the beach was considered "sissy" by this crowd. Off the waterfront dock was the only place to swim—besides we had no bathing trunks.

The first up was Fitz himself who stripped naked, climbed up on one of the tar-covered pilings, beat his chest and, with a Tarzan yell, jumped feet-first into the water.

He swam around the pier about a hundred yards to where the cement boat-launching area, was, then pulled himself up. He was dripping seaweed and green/black scum from the harbor. His pupils were large and his breath heavy.

"Man, you gotta swim fast 'cause there's sharks out there!"

"Oh, yeah, right," said Tommy, his second-in-command. "And explosive mines for the submarines."

I had by this time hunkered down behind a piling out of the wind. Fitz was a pretty tough guy but I could see him shivering from the cold. He was also spitting up thick phlegm; he looked a little green. Nobody else seemed particularly anxious to jump in.

"You're next," Fitz said, turning to Tommy.

"Yeah, well. I think I'll let Bubba go first. How about it, Bubba?"

Bubba, a sad-faced and corpulent thirteen-year old with a bad complexion, did not seem particularly excited about the idea.

"Come on, Bubba, what are you waiting for?"

Bubba backed away from the pier.

"You don't jump in, Bubba, we're going to throw you in," Tommy yelled.

Bubba stripped and made his jump, not from the top of the piling, but from the side of the pier. Within minutes everyone had made his jump, although none actually *stayed* in or swam more than the necessary strokes to get back to the boat launch.

"Come on, kid,' Tommy said. "You're next."

"Me?" I asked.

"Is there anyone else standing around with their clothes on lookin' stupid?"

"But I can't swim," I said. "I don't know how."

"Yeah, well. Guess you don't have time to learn swimming, with all the studying you do at the Catholic school, right. All that Latin and theology and stuff, huh, kid?" said Fitz in a mock-friendly voice.

"Yeah, that's right."

"You're an altar boy, too, right, kid?

"Yeah, that's right," I said.

"See?" Fitz said to the rest, as if talking to a class of rather dumb students. "Mikey is a Catholic boy who has lots of responsibilities. He can't just be jumping off piers like you knuckleheads. He's special."

"Yeah," said Tommy. "Special."

"Yeah," agreed the rest of the gang with a conspiratorial glint in their collective eyes. "Special."

They rushed me and, before I knew it, I was sailing in the air, off the dock and headed down to the cold, oily water. When I hit, I sank. Down, down in the cloudy ocean, seaweed and garbage and translucent engine oil sliding past my eyes. I held my breath and began flailing and kicking toward the pier. But, before I could reach the surface, I had opened my mouth and taken in some of the foul water. Spluttering and coughing I finally made it to the surface, expecting help, rescue, but no one was there. I swung my arms and kicked, then settled into the best imitation of a breast stroke that I could manage. My brain was frozen in a single thought: *survive!*

Somehow, after minutes which seemed like an hour, I managed to make it to the concrete boat slip, and the hands of the other boys were there to pull me up. I knocked them away. Then I hit Tommy a sucker punch, a hard right-cross to the jaw.

"Why, you little punk!" he yelled and then cocked his fist to hit me back.

"Naw, Tommy! Leave off," ordered Fitz. "You had it coming."

He handed me his jacket. "Here, Mikey, put this over your shoulders. We'll go down to the beach and light a fire. You did okay, kid," he said. "Just like your uncle in the war."

I swallowed back my tears then, and I put on his leather jacket. I followed them, marching down to the beach, pretending I was a Marine, that I had landed with the rest of the troops and that, unlike my uncle, I would survive.

DANNY

SOME CHILDREN ARE ANGELIC from birth: the golden hair, the beautiful wide eyes, the smile that brightens the entire face, the open personality. Even people who don't like babies stop and gaze at them in wonder. My neighbor Danny was that kind of child. And when other children passed through the "terrible twos" and the "fearsome fours," Danny retained his remarkable disposition and looks. He was the honored child in both our families, even though both his mother and mine pretended to have no favorites. I was two years younger than Danny and his sister Karen was a year younger. We had the typical diseases, the awkwardness of children, the pale Irish skin and skinny bodies. Our looks were average, our charm fleeting. We always knew that, compared to Danny, we were lesser beings.

But Karen and I loved Danny and were never jealous. It was hard not to love him with his dark curly hair and green eyes. His body was that of a young Greek god, perfectly proportioned and muscled even though he seldom exercised, except for shooting baskets in our backyard or throwing knives against the old maple tree. He smiled often and he had a gentle and musical voice. He was a natural leader and always made the rules in our childhood games.

By the summer of sixth grade he had girlfriends. Girls just kind of drifted over to his house to play. Sometimes they were his sister's friends; sometimes they were girls from school who came especially to see Danny. Always they ended up in Danny's room playing games he invented out of curiosity and daring. Always they came back for more.

He had a large crab apple tree in his backyard and when the fruit got ripe we often pretended that the apples were hand grenades and played war games. Our sides were mostly boys, four or five to a battalion, but occasionally girls would join: Danny's sister because she was a tomboy, and usually some love-struck girl who jumped in simply because Danny was playing.

If you were hit by an apple then you were captured and had to go over to the opposite side. Danny's team always won and, after a while, it became boring. One day he decided that certain prisoners when taken would be tied up to the tree and then "interrogated." I was one of the first. And when Danny asked me in his best German accent, "Vy did jew cum to Berlin?" I immediately confessed that it was to fight his Nazi army and to help defeat them. He pretended to shoot me in the head, then untied me and let me go.

He then had his soldiers tie up Linda Jensen. Linda was about eleven then, I guess, the same age as Danny. After she was tied up, Danny checked the knots and made sure that they were secure. He began questioning her as usual but there was something slightly different. The German accent was still there, but I felt listening to him that the humor was gone and something else, maybe cruelty, had taken its place. No one else noticed, though, and he continued to question her. She laughed shyly at his questions. It was apparent that she was infatuated with him and enjoyed being in close proximity.

He had his face inches from her as he talked. Then he whispered, "Would you like to kiss me?" I didn't hear the response, but I saw them kiss but not as kids usually do. The kiss was sensual and prolonged. When it ended, he brushed his body against hers. Then he turned on his heel and announced to us all: "This girl is a spy. She's been lying, and hoping to use her wiles on me. She must be hanged."

He ordered two of the boys to get another piece of rope. He fastened a noose on the end and then looped it over one of the lower branches. None of the other kids actually thought that Danny was serious about hanging Linda. It was just another step in the make-believe of the war game. But I had a funny feeling about it and spoke to his sister. "What do you think, Karen?"

"I think we'd better help her escape," she said.

I got Danny to one side and started talking to him about the proposed hanging while his sister snuck over and began to untie the binding on Linda's hands.

Danny smiled at me as I explained to him that he really didn't want to put a noose around Linda's neck, that it was dangerous, that we might hurt her accidentally, that she'd tell and we'd all get into trouble. Meanwhile, I knew that Karen had time to release the hostage but I heard no one running away. I turned, and Linda was still there. Her bindings had been loosened but she was still standing stupidly by the tree.

Danny brushed past me and walked over to the apple tree. He put his hand on Linda's cheek and stroked it as a lover might. "You really don't want to run away, do you, Linda?"

Linda shook her head.

"I think everyone can go now," Danny said.

"Come on, Danny. We're playing a game," I said. "Let's have another battle with the apples."

"I'm tired of that game," Danny said, not taking his eyes off of Linda. "You guys beat it. Go back to the house and play Monopoly or something. You heard me. Beat it!" he snapped when nobody made a move.

There was something flat and smooth in his eyes which had replaced the absorbent quality one usually saw there. Karen and I turned away from those eyes, as if there was something coiled invisibly behind then at which we dared not look.

We left then, went up to the house and there in the kitchen had Toll House cookies and milk, then went to the living room to play Monopoly. I remember getting up from the game a couple of times to look out the window, and noticed that the ropes were gone from the tree. There no sounds coming from the empty back yard.

It wasn't until two days later that my mother said we weren't to play in the crab apple tree any more. "It's too dangerous," she said. "One of your little friends had a rope caught around her neck and almost died." My mother was a literal person, who would not have understood my reference to Danny's eyes and the light that had gone out of them, even if I had the words to describe them. Besides, when it came to Danny she harbored no thoughts peripheral to her singular affection.

Linda came around a couple of times after that. She was shy and withdrawn. She had an ugly bruise around her neck, and Danny studiously ignored her.

I asked her later about what had happened, and she told me that she couldn't tell. "Danny would get mad at me," she said.

I went into the house determined to tell Mom all I knew but before I could open my mouth she yelled," Look at all the mud on your shoes. Do you think I've got nothing better than to clean up after you all day? Why can't you be more like Danny?"

"You don't understand," I told her. "You don't know what Danny is really like. If you know half the things he...."

The next thing I knew I felt his hand on my shoulder. I hadn't heard him come up behind me. I turned and looked into his clear green eyes. He smiled at me and then spoke charmingly to my mother.

"It's okay, Mrs. H. We're going out to play now; aren't we, Mikey?"

"Then go play, for goodness sake!" she said shooing us out the door.

It was a clear autumn day. I remember the heavy odor of rotting apples, the murmuring of the bees, and Danny's bright smile as he led me down the walk and out to the crab apple tree.

DIAMONDS ARE FOREVER

IT IS LATE OCTOBER. The bright green of the baseball diamond is like an emerald, sculpted and pure. But I have no time today for art or poetry. It is the bottom of the ninth in the last game of the Series. Our team is down by two runs. There are two outs. I cheer as Dom DiMaggio hits a single. Jimmy Piersall brings a smile to my face as he finally walks after making the sign of the cross on the plate several times before each pitch and throwing off Bobby Hogue's timing. Now there is a man on first and second. Two out. The bottom of the ninth. And it's my turn at bat. My stomach tightens and I feel the eyes of the crowd on me as I get ready to come out of the batter's box.

"Come on, Mike, let's go! Let's go; you're up," the Manager barks at me from the dugout.

My palms are sweating even though it is a cool October day. The sky is cloudless; the field incredibly, eternally green. The fans are yelling my name. "Mike, Mike! Hit it down the pike. Mike, Mike! No strike!" Their voices roar like the ocean. They make a wave in the stands like the tide. "Mike, Mike! No strike!"

I choose my bat carefully. This is the most important day of my life. I will never forget this day. Nothing exists but now. It is the eternal now. The only now that will ever exist. My hands perspire. I wipe them on my pants. Now, now. Pitch it to me. STRIKE ONE! I didn't even see it; it was that fast. Hogue has been clocked at over 95 miles an hour. That's fast, brother. This time I'll watch it closer. Whew! That was close. BALL ONE! This guy is dangerous. Last season he busted two of my knuckles; had my hand in a cast for a month. Better be careful. Better move back...don't want to get hit by that ball. I can hear Berra chuckling behind me.

Whoomp! STRIKE TWO. Now that won't do. The crowd is quiet, holding its collective breath. Everyone is counting on me. Even my mother is up there somewhere, praying for her son. All my friends are up there hoping for the big hit. I can't afford to be scared. The pitcher throws the ball to first, to check the runner there. I say a little prayer. The fear leaves me. I see nothing but the pitcher now. I think of nothing but the ball. The pitcher winds up and throws. It is a fast ball, a curve, but I am so focused, so clear, so fearless, so concentrated that I can see each red stitch in the seam as the ball swirls towards me. I smile to myself and swing a god-almighty swing, and the bat smacks, connects with the ball right at the break between the seams, and the ball rises, rises in a high arc, up, up, up in the cloudless autumn sky. It does not hang there but goes on and out and up over the 37 foot-high left field wall.

Behind me, Curt Gowdy, who was calling the play-by-play, is on his feet in the press booth. He is pacing down up and down as he broadcasts to the folks at home listening on their radios. "Unbelievable. Absolutely incredible. Ted Williams step aside. Big Mike is in his stride! We are witnessing a bit of history today, folks. Big Mike has hit that ball well over 315 feet, over the highest left field wall in professional baseball, the fabled Green Monster, for an incredible three-run homer for the Red Sox win."

The fans roar as I coast past first base, lightly touch second, and still the ball is sailing. It may land someday, somewhere on the other side of Kenmore Square. I round third towards home, the other players giving me high fives as I head towards the dugout, the crowd on its feet cheering, and my mother: "Mike-ee, Mike-ee!" she yells.

"Hi, Mom," I wave.

I am in the dugout now but the crowd continues to roar. They want me. "Mike, Mike! We want Mike!" I come out and tip my hat to acknowledge their adoration. Then again I hear my mother's voice above the roar of the crowd.

"Mike-ee! Mike-ee! Come in now and wash up for supper. Your dad will be home soon."

I am nine years old. It is a gray October in my backyard. The grass is weed-choked and dusty. The air is cold with the north winds of autumn. Leaves are falling from the old pear tree. But I am content in my heart. I have done what I have done. The ball sails over the cobblestone streets of Boston, through the blue skies of all my days. And the perfect diamond of that field is in my mind whenever I choose to look for it. Diamonds are forever.

OCEAN DRIVE

THE TEN-MILE HORSESHOE LOOP that begins on Harrison Avenue and ends on mansion-lined Bellevue is a spectacular route. It fronts, on the one hand, the Atlantic coast at its most varied, rock-strewn and reefed diversity and, on the other, the gardens, walls and terraces of 19th century mansions of the Gilded Age.

In the Fifties the Sunday afternoon car ride was as common and non-negotiable as compulsory church attendance. After Mass and the heavy mid-day meal, the whole family piled into the Plymouth station wagon and headed out to the Ocean Drive, my Dad, Mom, my thirteen year-old sister and I, the eleven-year-old director in a film of his own making. Always, there was something new.

The seasons are very marked in Newport and in summer the maples with their helicopter seeds, the canopy of elms that formed great arches over Harrison Avenue (before the plague would eradicate them forever), the flowering dogwood, the oaks and the willows freshened the car as we drove with the windows down in those pre-air conditioned days past the fields with young colts and thoroughbred mares, past model farms where sheep and black Angus grazed, where neat cottages and gate houses fronted the road. Sometimes there was the excitement of Curt Gowdy or Red Barber on the radio, the sound of wooden bats connecting with baseballs. Always there was the smell of seaweed—poignant and sad as the cries of gulls.

In autumn there was the brilliant red of the oaks, the gold and russet of maples as the leaves turned and only evergreens and *rosa rugosa* stayed true to their summer green. There was the rich smell of apples in the air, a hint now and then of the arctic in the fading Indian summer as the grass slowly faded to brown, and geese began their migratory search for warmer climes. There were the sounds of football being played which echoed across the fields and the parks in the crisp salty air. Squirrels hurried across the road with acorns and pine cones to stash for the cold months ahead.

And while I am no longer tempted by the pleasures of winter (my blood now thinned by more than two decades in a tropical land), that season, too, was rich in association. The scraping of ice off the windshield, the long warm-up of the reluctant engine, the crisp, red-nosed walk to the car as the wind whistled up the driveway between our house and our neighbor's. On our drive down to visit the frozen ponds to see if anyone was skating, we passed the denuded but crystalline trees, the green and stately cypress, the fir and the pine. Then, out onto the Ocean Drive where rime-ringed rocks bordered the ocean, with the ocean itself contributing its frozen soap foam, while chill winds rocked the car and sent sweeps of snow across the road where it drifted, billowing up against the rock walls of the farms. In the fields beyond was an occasional white rabbit, metamorphosed from her summer brown by solstitial changes certain as ice storms.

My father loved to drive, and there was such pleasure to it in those un-trafficked day when the mechanics of the internal combustion engine were completely understood by most good drivers, and maintenance was largely done in one's own driveway or garage: draining the oil, lubricating the chassis, cleaning the sparkplugs, adjusting the points, or loosening the carburetor screw while my sister or I (in a proud moment of honor behind the wheel) responded to our father's signals: "Give it some gas...okay, now let off." The rotation of tires, the adjusting of brakes, putting on and taking off snow chains, all formed a part of a good driver's curriculum.

So the car was always a maintained and known entity. And driving was a process not limited to steering, acceleration and braking, but involved careful attention to the alternation of sound in the mixture of air and fuel, of pistons rising and falling, the hum of tires: hands sensitive to any imbalance in the front end (even letting go of the steering wheel to check the drift) caused by under-inflation of the tires or problems with alignment. Men knew their machines and listened. They felt the idiosyncrasies of the car, noted them as they drove, with a deep attention in their bones to each tic and murmur no matter what the scenery, the conversation, or the music on the radio. My father was always attentive to the larger issue much as a doctor smiling and chatting to his patient listens with a deeper awareness to the resonance of the stethoscope and the problems its sounds might portend.

In an island community of less than 30,000, a businessman and store owner such as my Dad knew a goodly number of the residents. All his parents' and grandparents' friends, all his extended family of cousins, aunts and uncles, all the cops, firemen, teachers, businessmen, members of the Holy Name Society and the

Knights of Columbus. He knew all the politicians, elected and otherwise, the city clerks and the building inspectors. He knew all the "colored people" by name, a tiny population conspicuous by its small number. He knew the wealthy Anglo-Saxon estate owners as well as their Irish and Portuguese gardeners who often came to his shop, the well-known Newport Seed, Bulb and Supply Company. He knew the secretaries from the downtown offices, the ferry captains, the lighthouse keeper, the snow plowman, the doctors from Newport Hospital and the nurses. He knew the Navy Base commander and professors from Salve Regina College. I mention all this because the greeting of each of them was also an integral part of any Sunday drive with my father. In those days before multi-tasking became a household word, my father could listen diagnostically to the car engine, keep peace between my sister and me in the back seat, carry on a conversation with my mother, catch the score of the Red Sox game on the softly murmuring radio, and every ten minutes or so greet a neighbor or resident with a wave, a shouted greeting, a toot of the horn, a respectful nod and--at least once every half hour a resigned stop by the side of the road as the other car pulled alongside to discuss more fully the repairs on the Mount Hope Bridge, the boys fighting in Korea, the politics of Senator Green, the up-coming visit of Ike, or the price of fuel oil. Sometimes the stops were more personal: to commiserate on the death of a loved one, or congratulate a coach on the success of his team, or a father whose son won a scholarship. Our Sunday drive of twelve miles was much like the journey of Odysseus, a short one geographically, which seemed to take forever on those never-ending Sunday afternoons. At some of these stops we would pile out of the car and, after dire warnings from Mom to be careful lest we be swept away by the waves and lost forever, we'd climb over the sea wall to meander among the sea-cast boulders looking for crabs, for periwinkles and mussels, for interesting shells or driftwood to cart home in the trunk of our Plymouth.

Our Plymouth always shone in the Sunday light as if just driven off the showroom floor. And this was because in fair weather, Saturday afternoons were Simonize times in which the car was soaped down, rinsed with a hose, dried with towels. This preliminary cleansing was followed by the application of Simonize or Turtle Wax in small, manageable areas in a circular motion until it dried and a white film appeared. It could not be allowed to dry in the sun, which was why Simonize jobs were usually done underneath the shade of large trees. The area where the wax was applied could not be allowed to dry in the air. It needed to be rubbed in until the film appeared. Then the white dullness was buffed out vigorously with a chamois cloth to reveal the brilliant shining color of the original paint job. It was a labor-intensive job requiring "elbow grease," as my Dad used to say, that combination of sheer will, unrelenting labor and vigor, which few contemporary tasks now demand except perhaps using a post hole digger out on a ranch with rocky terrain. Certainly there is not the remotest comparison with today's modern "quick shine" applications. A forty-one year-old father and an eleven year-old son working side by side under a spreading chestnut tree might complete the job, including the vacuuming the interior and bleaching the white wall tires in just under three hours. But the results were worth it because the boy would earn the privilege of a short, supervised drive behind the wheel past other boys his age who would wave or even whistle at the showroom shine of the carefully buffed car. Now it was ready for the Sunday drive.

Which...by the way, continued, in an endless series of impressions as we rounded the Castle Rock Coast Guard Station, and entered the broad sweep of the ocean view. For me, as for such diverse writers as Stephen King, Marcel Proust, Ranier Maria Rilke and Joyce Carol Oates, those preteen years are still my most vivid, and I owe to them my awareness of self, and my sense of place and belonging. They have led me to the belief that life is less understood or even intrinsically meaningful (this is to say capable of being understood) than it is a series of images and impressions themselves unintelligible whose significance derives from the narratives we shape. Like Stephen King, I believe that the things we fear at age eleven are still with us and we have come not to fear them less, but merely to have dulled those early impressions into floating anxieties or the occasional early morning dread, nameless and undefined.

I know that at age eleven I understood nothing and felt everything. I know that I had no metaphysical language sufficient for what I felt and that I descended into long brooding silences during those walks along the shore with my sister when we were ostensibly hunting flotsam treasures. She was coming to the end of her appreciation for the Sunday drives and at thirteen was thinking about her friends, junior high boys, and more interesting ways to pass her Sunday afternoons then seated in the back seat of a Plymouth with her kid brother, or walking the littoral while her father talked with adults who were dull and boring. For me, during those walks along the shore I was a Navy captain on a destroyer looking through the mist for the telltale scope of a Nazi submarine. Or, I was adrift on the ocean of time itself wondering about the source of the universe and whether there was a God, and if my existence had any meaning in the world. When I returned to the car with my sister at the end of one of these walks, the silence often persisted and the conversation of my parents seemed superficial and irrelevant. It seemed to me that language was a tool to unravel the mysteries of life, if they could be unraveled. Or, if not, then language existed for the purpose of creating my own narratives which would give some cohesive shape to the stream of broodings and fantasies, images and existential puzzlings which plagued my waking hours.

But language was a blunt, awkward, highly imperfect tool. Language as spoken around me did not exalt the human spirit, it trivialized it. People spoke of other people, or events, or the season, with the resignation of the given which could not be enhanced or illuminated. We are what we are and the world is what it is, they seemed to be saying. No more. No less. And this to me was a diminution of all I saw and felt. I knew language had to do more; otherwise there was no point in using it. Thus, for most of that summer, much to the consternation of my mother, I refused to speak. I communicated by gestures and grunts. My father was amused and tried to tease me out of it. My sister, busy with her friends, ignored me. I spent whole days in the woods, walking the cliffs above the sea, writing in my journal. I also spent hours in the evening with the dictionary, copying words, sounding them out, moving from one word to the other as the meaning of one demanded knowledge of another and still another word.

Silent then in the backseat as our glistening blue 1954 Plymouth made the turn to mansion-lined Bellevue Avenue, I waited for my father to give us a history of one mansion or another: describe the architecture, unravel the mystery of the owners, relate anecdotes about the men who worked to maintain it. Minutes later, as we approached his store next to the Newport Casino (and now the Tennis Hall of Fame), he gave us a bit of tennis lore; then a shy tease as we passed La Forge, a sophisticated luncheon spot, that it was a shame we didn't care much for ice cream, and my mother claiming that it was just as well because "silent Mike" in the backseat, and Sheila's Bermuda shorts rendered us both ineligible for formal desserts.

But my father was no ogre, so out to East Main Road in Middletown where in the farm belt that bordered the city, among dairy cows and corn, was the Newport Creamery. The Creamery not only had the best ice cream in the State of Rhode Island and Providence Plantations if not all of New England, but it also had a wonderful concoction called the "Awful-Awful" a triple-rich milkshake of quality ice cream and milk with none of the dairy cream removed. These shakes were so rich that if you could drink two, the management would give you a third one for free—a test the Rogers' and De La Salle football linemen sometimes passed in the pre-season effort to gain weight.

And then home, satiated for a time while Mom and Dad took a nap, Sheila and I read, or she called her friends while I read (boys didn't chat on phones in those days—only girls). Then, grilled cheese sandwiches and tea as we gathered around a black and white 20-inch T.V. to listen to Bishop Fulton J. Sheen tell us that "Life Is Worth Living" in his eponymous broadcast.

And yet, I should not be so glib here when speaking about Bishop Sheen. A conservative Thomistic theologian who preached an anti-Communist message just a trifle less radical than Sen. Joseph McCarthy, Bishop Sheen enshrined the nuclear family in its last hurrah "(The family that prays together, stays together); but he also had something that I wished to emulate. He had a presence. He swept on the stage dressed in a black cassock and stiff Roman collar, while a black cape lined with red silk flowed behind him. His face was handsome and kindly, his hair silver with maturity and his voice...ah, his voice: melodious, resonant, and replete with imagery, metaphor, allusions from the classics and the Bible, and quotations from the Church Fathers. But most of all, what one heard as one listened to Fulton Sheen was a deep conviction: that the soul was no fiction, that ideas were real, and that language was a proven way to give shape to the chaos of the world.

Later I was to hear Robert Frost and Dylan Thomas read their poetry aloud, and both the workman-like iambs of Frost and the rich deliciousness of vowels in Thomas' poems convinced me of the power of spoken language to restore wonder to observation and colorful elaboration to the black and white of the page. All of which made me want to become a writer who spoke. I didn't know what that would translate into exactly: a preacher, an orator, a poet, a teacher? Other models soon presented themselves in the speeches of Knute Rockne to the Notre Dame team at half time, the homilies of the Protestant minister

Norman Vincent Peale, the speech to Congress after December 7, 1941 by President Roosevelt.

At any rate, the days of silence ended with the start of school, and rich with language, bursting with language, my earlier reticence had its revenge. I had suddenly developed a stammer. At first incipient, a hardly noticeable tic in the elision of certain consonants, it now developed into a full scale disability extending to the basic vowels that left me tongue-tied and red-faced whether answering a question in the classroom or talking to a junior high girl. Hormones ran amuck as I turned twelve and I was angry, frustrated, and bursting with language which obstinately refused to come.

NEWPORT, 1955

MY CLEAREST MEMORY OF MY father is on a late spring morning, probably May, when the jonquils were already blooming and the green spears of the tulips had appeared. My father was out in the front yard trimming the grass around the flower beds.

When church ladies walked past on their way home from late Mass, my father tipped his straw hat and mumbled a hello. I say "mumble" because, although he knew most of the people who lived on our street, there were many in the neighborhood that he did not know by name. Sometimes for twenty minutes there would be the snip, snip of the grass shears followed by "Mornin' Miz Quinn. Mornin' Miz Umm-hum. Mornin' Miz Sullivan."

Clip, clip. "Get me a flat of Babies' Breath for the border, Mike." Clip, clip.

"Ah, mornin' Miz Taylor. Mornin' Miz Umm-umm. Mr. Um-umm. How're the children?"

He had been up for five hours at this point. He always rose at 6:30, had coffee at the R.I. Lunch so he wouldn't wake my mother, read a bit of the Sunday paper there, and then returned in time for our awakening and the Children's Mass at eight.

He dressed quite formally and conservatively. Black shoes, a grey suit, blue tie. Sometimes when he felt particularly sporty he would wear grey slacks, red tie, with a yellow sweater vest under a blue suit jacket. In spring, he always had a straw hat; in winter, a felt fedora. He looked a bit like Frank Sinatra, especially when he tilted the brim of the hat in the rakish way of the popular crooner.

The year is 1955. Most of the streets in our neighborhood are tree-lined: old oaks, maples with their helicopter seeds, and enormous elm trees which in summer, growing on both sides of the street, formed a canopy which made a boy feel like he was in a forest just recently hacked out the forest. But of course, there was little recent about Newport, as the boy had learned by the age of twelve.

It was an early settlement of exiles from England and from the banished followers of Anne Hutchinson and Roger Williams in the 1630s. Likely, its history was even older. Despite the fact that Longfellow's poem about the Old Stone Mill and the early Norse settlers has since been discounted, there is sufficient evidence that the port was not unknown to early seafarers. Everywhere you went on the island, there was history. The 17th Century British coat of arms was still hanging in Trinity Church, and the pew where George Washington sat was marked with a bronze plaque. Bishops Berkeley's organ was in this church as well. Near the ocean was his home Whitehall. Portuguese Jews displaced by the Lisbon earthquake in the 17th century had settled here and were buried in the graveyard of Touro Synagogue, the oldest temple in the New World. Richard Henry Dana lived not far from here, as had Gilbert Stuart, the Channings and even Roger Williams for a while.

Like all really interesting towns, Newport had its seamy side as well. Although nowadays it has been largely gentrified, in 1955 there was still the Gas House Gang, the Irish toughs of the Fifth Ward, the sailors and the Marines in the rough bars along Thames (pronounced then in the English way, "Tems") Street, the Negro neighborhood, the rough and tumble docks, Long Wharf, the cinder lots and broken pavement near the railroad depot, the vacant lots and haunted houses, Tim the Ragpicker, and the Crazy Lady on Carroll Avenue.

But there was also the Newport of the Ocean Drive and the Cliff Walk where one could see the magnificent homes of the last of the robber barons of the 1890s: the Duponts, the Rockefellers, the Pierponts, the Morgans and the Vanderbilts. It was the vacation spot of presidents and the locus of the summer White House for Dwight D. Eisenhower and later for John F. Kennedy.

My grandfather was an Irish gardener at one of these incredibly grand summer mansions. His position and interchanges with other gardeners gave me access to some of the most gorgeous vistas on the island and entry at a very early age to some of the most lavish specimens of the *haut monde*.

By the age of ten I was familiar with the Copley portraits in the front hall as I brought in fresh-cut flowers to the Madame. I had seen Dresden china set out for breakfast. I had scrubbed Venetian marble steps before lunch, and had polished Rodin bronzes out on the front lawns. The summer of my twelfth year, at my father's intercession, I was hired by T.J. Brown, a landscape contractor who provided the gardeners with additional help in the summers, mowing the acres of lawn, trimming the arbors, hedges and shrubs, and raking the half mile of winding gravel drive which ran up to the front door of the most humble of these forty room "cottages."

Early morning it was my job to smooth these long (and two cars' wide) gravel drives. I slowly dragged and pushed a long-handled wooden rake over the deep gravel, over to one side, then the other, two steps back, then again. Drug, push, drag, push. Step back, cross over. It was a two-hour job with plenty of time to listen and observe. The early mists rising from the trees, the sounds of flickers and wrens, occasionally a song bird, were part of my morning. The bleat of sheep from a hill off in the distance, the fog horns of destroyers out in Narragansett Bay, the thin scrape of the rake were my summer music. Had my parents wished me to become a poet, they could not have planned it better.

Always on these summer mornings there was the sense of the world being born again. There was time (in the rhythmic, automatic movements of the great wooden rake) to conjure images of old seafarers, of Puritans and merchants, of Narragansett Indians and fiery-eyed clerics, of Vikings and longboats, and to hear in the sounds of the countryside, in rhythms of the rake and my breathing, the old iambs and dactyls of the race. There was time (in the motes of dust dancing in the sun) to ponder, and sometimes the thoughts were so deeply intertwined with the beauty of the natural world around me, the solitude and peace of the island, that I could not have said what I was thinking, nor could I have told you then that I was happy. The feelings, the thoughts, were only half-formed and far too ephemeral to articulate. Today I would say that I learned what epiphany was on those mornings: "the intersection of the timeless with time" in Eliot's concise description. I knew intuitively what I would later understand in the prose of Emerson and the poetry of Wordsworth; I was already a young Transcendentalist, and I knew that all that I beheld was full of blessings.

My father had his own business. The son of a gardener, he had put aside the blue collar of the previous generations of Irish and put on the suit and tie of an entrepreneur. He owned Frank Hogan's Newport, Seed, Bulb and Supply Co., a business which furnished farmers and professional gardeners from Rhode Island to Massachusetts' North Shore and then down the Cape with the seeds, bulbs, fertilizers, machines and implements of farming and gardening. A disciplined autodidact, he knew the Latin names of all the plants, flowers and trees which grew in New England, as well as the common names, both general and regional. His knowledge was exhaustive and encyclopedic. His was as fascinating as Linnaeus in his experiments and lectures, whether helping to develop the Kearns' Big Boy chrysanthemum or patiently explaining to an elderly patron the anomaly of the black tulip. Horticulturalist, botanist and businessman, he was elected Secretary of the National Association of Professional Gardeners in his thirties and held the position to the end of his life.

Ours was a Catholic family and my sister and I were raised in the strictest of that tradition. Catholicism was not the majority religion of Newport at the time; nevertheless, it was all-encompassing—especially in the largely Irish confines of the Fifth Ward. We prayed together as a family each night, saying the rosary for the conversion of Russia, and for peace in the world. We dressed in white to carry flowers in the May Procession; made our First

Communion and confirmation, and attended Catholic schools. I was also an altar boy, proud of my careful Latin, and convinced at an early age of a calling to the priesthood. My mother was a daily communicant and a member of the Rosary and Scapular Society, and my father so devoted to the Blessed Mary that he would not own a car unless it was painted blue, Our Lady's color. In this Irish neighborhood, even the skeptical would not crack a smile at the extremity of his devotion.

Our education was disciplined and rigid. Mine even more, I think, than that of my sister because I was wilder and more spirited. I remember once in the eighth grade placing a mixture of sugar and salt peter on the principal's window sill during one lunch period. This heady mixture (the ingredients of a primitive gunpowder) when lit, explodes like the whump of those Civil War hand-held camera flashes in a burst of smoke, leaving behind a remarkable black by-product of combustion.

As I was getting the match out of my pocket to light it, the other boys suddenly ran away. Denouncing them for cowards, I touched the match to the mixture on the window sill, just as the principal opened the window and stuck her head out to see what was going on. WHOOSH-WHUMP went the gunpowder and Sister Mary Joachim's white starched wimple turned black in an instant and her pale skin mottled with rage. I remember the sore knuckles, the many days spent after school clapping erasers and sweeping classroom floors. I remember the feeling of being an outlaw, and wondered what would become of me.

This incident was just another in a long history. I had been caught spilling red finger paint down the front of

41

Mary Newbury's dress in the 3rd grade. I was caught using a ruler for a baton and vigorously directing my 4th grade class in the "Star Spangled Banner" after the teacher, who had briefly stepped out of the room, unexpectedly returned. In the 5th grade, I was caught writing "Sister Monica is a Honaker" on Donnie Gill's notebook. Retaliation was swift and terrible. Always.

"What makes you do these things? my mother would ask, bewildered and angry at the latest explicit documentary of my delinquency. I stood silent, sometimes with what was interpreted as a defiant smirk on my face. But the fact is, I had no answer then. I simply did not know. Now I'd guess that it was an inherited dislike for regimentation, arbitrary rules, and unquestioning obedience. After all, my grandparents left the Old World to get away from all that. This was America, for goodness sake, and Newport, supposedly the cradle of intellectual and religious freedom. Most likely, I had also heard by this time a dozen stories from my grandfather on the Easter Rising of 1916, and would have felt closer to that tradition than I did to the unquestioning allegiance to the rules of priests and nuns who, I would have learned early on, did not to support the Irish in their efforts to overthrow British tyranny.

In addition to my grandfather's revolutionary narratives which enriched my imagination, like every boy my age I knew even more stories about troops in World War II from magazine stories, and accounts of veterans. We were all "war babies" and were enmeshed in the war and post-war recovery. Likes most boys I was fascinated by such tales and incorporated them in my fantasies. Many an afternoon I pretended to be Sgt. Audie Murphy assaulting a tank single-handed or General Patton leading his troops across Italy. I was also vitalized by exploration whether of deep woods, abandoned houses, worked-out quarries, or old fortifications. It was in such places that my fantasies could be acted out on a real life stage with my closest friends as active participants and audience. It was there, too, that the first blood was shed in action, the first bones broken, the first lessons of camaraderie and courage learned.

FORT ADAMS

BEFORE THE JAZZ FESTIVALS, the condominiums, the gentrification of Thames Street, the Beds and Breakfasts, and the Bridge that let the tourists and New York investors turn my hometown into a theme park, there was another Newport. Shrouded by fog, slowed by cobblestone streets, full of abandoned mysterious mansions, turreted and dark, it was a town that held history as mysteriously as the true wine in some misplaced Medieval grail.

It was in this town at the unreflecting age of twelve that I traveled with my best buddies Bob Beebe and Tommy Gough by bicycle up the broad stretch of Harrison Avenue headed for the Ocean Drive. Our destination was an old fort, long-abandoned, which looked out over the cliffs of Narragansett Bay, guarding the entrance to the harbor.

It was a place that we were forbidden to go. Honeycombed with flooded tunnels in danger of imminent collapse, the ten-acre fort was full of unexploded shells, rusted ammunition, broken pipes, and empty buildings where sailors on shore leave (it was said) took unsuspecting virgins, and where escaped convicts had in fact been tracked down and, soaked by fog and rain and cold, surrendered peacefully to the law.

On this particular day in October, when the fog lay heavy on the roads, we cut off to the dirt path, bordered by knee-high, seed-scattering weeds, feeling the salt dew soak our pants and the gonad-smashing bike seats setting back puberty a year. We suffered it all, as good soldiers would, because we were planning a defensive attack on the amphibious German force which even now was steaming up the harbor threatening the town.

When we reached the parade ground of the old fort we cut saplings and pretended they were M-1s. We paraded for a bit under my orders either because Bob and Tommy were less argumentative or (as I believed) the leadership qualities of the Irish were inimitable. Then I gave the order that the M-1s were now Thompson sub-machine guns, far more satisfying weapons, capable of annihilating whole platoons as we set off through the darkened half-flooded tunnels, clotted with debris of old storms and vandals, and killed the Germans who had already come ashore in black rubber boats and who were, from the ugly leers as their faces rictored in death, stopped in the nick of time from attacking our sisters. Terrible, black-shirted, lightning bolt-epauletted Nazis were quickly dispatched to the world of Hades, so now we rested with army canteens of Kool-Aid and Camels and Old Golds stolen from our parents, and planned our next assault.

At the highest point of the fort was a cannon emplacement called Battery O'Shea. Overgrown with weeds, its rusted gun emplacements were mounted on top of a grass-covered hill. The hill was deceiving, however, because it was hollow. Below and inside was an empty ammunition park, big as an airplane hangar, which could be accessed by a rusted iron door ten feet high. We discovered that if we both pulled on the door together, our combined strength would serve to get it open. And, in the process of opening, the rusted hinges let forth a mournful sound that echoed out over the Bay like a foghorn.

Picture us then, planning our next attack. The German fleet coming up to the entrance of the Bay. We, the local rangers, having taken out the advance troop, were now sending signals to the American destroyers in the harbor. Tommy and I climbed up on the seats of our bikes so that we could both reach up and hang from the iron door and then, letting our bikes drop away, swing from the door together. Oooom-oooom, the deep base-throated voice bellowed out of the eerie fog over the hill and across the cold waters. Each time we swung, the heavy door gained momentum and, on the third pass, Tommy fell off and the door continued forward with only me aboard and my thumb hanging off the far side where it was sliced almost in half by the rusted metal of the door-jam, and blood jetted out like that of a bullfighter caught in the femoral by a horn. I dropped to the ground, too stunned by what had happened to feel pain, but sickened when I saw the white flash of bone beneath the skin and the scrap of flesh that was once my thumb hanging dawn in a wet flap.

Tommy and Bob, with instincts true to the breed of summer soldiers and sunshine patriots, or perhaps just fearful that they would be blamed, jumped on their bikes and took off down the hill. I reached in my pocket and took out the handkerchief I always carried (one of three things a gentleman always had, my father counseled—I forget the other two), wrapped the wound tight and mounted my bike. The ride home, about a mile or so, was one of panic because my pants were soaked by wet grass, my shirt covered in blood, and the injury surely in need of some outside attention which would mean a trip to our nearsighted local sawbones whose ministrations were as painful as most injuries.

But beneath all this, or perhaps on top of it, was the slowly lifting fog, the splash of color in the harbor as the sun threw its sparkling mantle across the Bay, the cool drip-soaked rush beneath the elm trees, and the feeling— not terrible just desolate—that I was alone. I was alone with my pain, with the blood, the white bone, the jet spray of my heart pump as my skinny legs peddled the '55 Schwinn Hornet home. Tommy and Bob had left me out of panic and fear. And even home, the place that I was headed, because there was no other close by, would—I suspected—not be a haven of solace or sympathy. Punished by the fates, I would be drubbed again by Mom for breaking rules, ruining my clothes, and racking up still another doctor's bill. Alone, alone, the outlaw child.

The feeling passed quickly. By the time I turned into the gravel drive of the white cottage I called home, the tears were already streaming down my face. Fantasizing that I would lose my thumb, that I would die from blood loss, helped me in the performance which was calculated to avoid a beating.

"What happened NOW!" my mother shouted as I staggered into the kitchen.

"I got hurt, up at Battery O'Shea...."

"Blood, blood!" she shouted as I stood there dripping through my improvised bandage. "All over my just-waxed floor! Over to the sink with that mess, you...." She snatched me by the shoulder. "And just what were you doing at that place? I've told you and told you, time and time again...."

"We were just playing and...."

"Was there rust?" she asked. "Was there rust on what cut you?"

"Yes. But why...."

"Oh, Jesus, Mary and Joseph! Lockjaw! You just wait here."

She called my father at work and together they took me to the half-blind octogenarian doctor, my father silent and grim, my mother regaling me the whole way with descriptions of the horrible death caused by blood poisoning where the jaw locks tight and the patient dies in spastic convulsions strangling on his own tongue.

We rushed into the doctor's office where he was roused from his midmorning nap. Grouchy and maladroit, he proceeded to clean the wound, give me a dozen stitches and a tetanus shot, all of which procedures caused more pain than the accident itself.

"Why do you DO these things to me?" wailed my mother as the doctor drew his thick needle through my torn flesh. "Why...to me?"

"You cause your mother a great deal of misery, boy," said the doctor, grunting as he hit bone, and then pulled the needle out to have a second go at it.

"Oww!" I cried out, the tears welling despite my attempt to be stoic. I felt like telling him to pay attention to his work and not be distracted by my mother's hysterics. But the two of them were getting along fine. It was almost as if they were enjoying it.

"And you think THAT hurts, do you? Well think of the pain your mother's had to put up with. First when you were born...."

"Oh, do you remember, doctor?" my mother asked. "Eight hours of labor and finally the cesarean."

"I remember it well. During a blackout it was. War-time and the generators wouldn't kick in. And there was this bucko headed out sideways. He almost killed you, no doubt of it."

"And then the chicken pox," added my mother, warming up now that she had a sympathetic ear. "The mumps, the fall from the garage roof when he was pretending to fly, the accident with the knife when he thought he was Jim Bowie, stepping on a broken bottle on the beach, crashing his bike into a tractor trailer....What does he DO these things to me?"

"He's a trial, no question there," the doctor said, giving the knot in the last stitch a final vicious twist. "Seems like he's made it his life's work to make you miserable."

We walked to the car and my father put his arm around me.

"You know your mother is easily upset, son. Why do you so these things to her?"

Jesus, I thought. From him, too. Is everyone crazy here? I was the one who got hurt. I was the one who was abandoned by my friend. I was the one who hand was used as a practice quilt for a purblind geriatric. Doing things to HER! Give me a break.

"Listen," I said. "I don't suppose I could have a cigarette?"

"Jesus, Mary and Joseph!" my mother said coming out the door of the emergency room just as I made my ill-time request. "Cigarettes! What next? Even the prodigal son was repentant."

I was quite on the way home. Drain, I suppose, of tears, of blood, of any hope of being understood or of receiving sympathy. They didn't give kids pain pills in those days, and the local anesthetic had worn off halfway through the stitching procedure, so I was feeling kind of bad. But below this pain, the throbbing ache in the hand, the weakness, the nausea, was that desolation again. Sitting in the back seat of our '52 Plymouth, breathing in the sick car smell of stale cigarette smoke from my father's Old Golds and the even sicker odor of the Lily of the Valley perfume my mother wore, I felt alone. How could I even be related to these people? What was I even doing in this town? I didn't belong here. I was alone, a stranger, a creature who somehow appeared here, brushed against people, but was not really one of them. Alone. Alone. And I knew then that I would always be. Oh, I would learn how to get along well enough and sometimes, assuming a virtue that I did not have, would come close to connecting with another human being. But behind even the most cherished friendship, the most genuine love, was that cold fog, the drip from the elm trees, the desolation. At first it was a place I fled from, sometimes in sports, sometimes in drink, sometimes in marathon conversations with poets that lasted until dawn. But it became a place I could not truly escape.

"Every tree," Rilke once wrote, "is the first tree of one's childhood." As a writer I have learned to return to that place, not in fear and trembling anymore, but in expectation that like a certain desert cactus which holds in its century of solitude the promise of a single white blossom, that place is also the truest one for me, the place where all trivia is stripped away and what's left is the steady pulse of gestation. I have learned that not only will this gestation not kill me (as the earlier one apparently almost killed my mother) but will with its monsters and angels pull me from myself so that I can become new again.

When the poet William Stafford died a few years ago, I went back and re-read his work. He was an accessible and kindly poet whose words continue to inform the best part of my literary memories. But of all the poems this gentle soul wrote, the one that feels truest to me is also the one that seems most cold, most desolate. Yet, this desolation, I suspect was what gave him the lever with which he moved us all. The poem is called "Ask Me" and here are a few lines from it:

> Some time when the river is ice ask me
> mistakes I have made. Ask me whether
> what I have done is my life. Others
> have come in their slow way into
> my thought, and some have tried to help
> or to hurt: ask me what difference
> their strongest love and hate has made.
> I will listen to what you say.
>
> You and I can turn and look
> at the silent river and wait....
> What the river says, that is what I say.

THE COLONEL

TENNIS IS SO POPULAR these days and so much a part of the average teenager's sports' experience, that it is difficult for most of them to imagine a time when it was not. Yet, in the post-war period and the Fifties of my childhood, tennis was considered more a rich man's sport played at country clubs and exclusive resorts. Competitive singles was largely a sport for the male sex and, although women had been competing for years at Wimbledon and other international venues, most were amateurs and the few professionals who did compete got paid so little it was laughable. It wasn't until Billie Jean King's assertiveness in 1967 and the Virginia Slim tournaments of the Seventies that the sport opened up for a generation of Chris Everts and Steffi Grafs, and finally grew to include the million-dollar players like Venus and Serena Williams who changed the sport forever making it the dream of every athletic boy and girl.

The courts in my hometown of Newport, RI, were mostly off-limits to working class kids like me: the excellent grass center courts and the red clay courts of the Newport Casino where the National Doubles Championships were held, were open only to wealthy members who paid a hefty annual fee. The courts at the Newport Country Club were restricted to those few rich families who were members, as were those at the even more exclusive Bailey's Beach. At the Brenton Village Navy facility inside Fort Adams, there were courts for officers and their dependents but these were not accessible to locals. Both composition and clay courts were available at Salve Regina College but only for registered students and faculty. So that left two casually-maintained asphalt courts at the city venue called Murphy Park on Carroll Avenue where, during the summer, students home from college would bang away in lusty volleys and dominate the courts in rugged camaraderie.

A twelve year-year old working at a summer job, I had little interest in tennis. To me, pickup games of basketball and football were more fun and more interesting. I played basketball at Murphy Park and at the YMCA, and in the prolonged light of New England summer evenings practicing foul shots along in the backyard with a hoop hung from the front of our garage. As fall approached and the football season began, I'd play touch games with my friends and rougher tackle games with boys from uptown in the same park that abutted the tennis area. On occasion we might glance over at the courts if a particularly cute coed was playing doubles. Sometimes we would head over to the water fountain close by to get a drink and watch a game or two. "Love-fifteen. Love-thirty. Deuce." We had no idea what this absurd scoring method could signify. It was remote from our experience, as were the crisp white shorts, the spotless tennis shoes, and the white sports shirts that were *de rigeur* in those days. We were ragamuffins, I suppose; heady youth, and tennis seemed effete, subtle, complex and sophisticated—more like an elaborate dance than a sport, or a dance to which we would never be invited.

So, it came as a surprise to me when an Army colonel who lived up the street from us, began talking about tennis one day with my Dad. "Does the boy play?" I heard him ask. "No," my Dad said, "but he loves sports and plays basketball, baseball, football." "Well," replied the Colonel, "if he ever wants a lesson tell him to stop by. I was an Army champion in my day."

Later my Dad would mention it and when I replied that I thought it was a sissy game, he began to tell me of some of the great players of the day: Poncho Gonzalez, Jack Kramer, Ken Rosewall, but the names meant little to me. However, I did admire the Colonel who had great stories to tell about the War which was not too distant in memory. My father's brother Harry had died in the Ardennes Forest of Belgium in January, 1945 during the last German push. A Little League baseball field in our neighborhood carried his name. War games in the local woods were still very much a part of our youthful pastimes. So, on a Saturday afternoon, home from a half-day's work with a landscape company, I stopped by to talk to Colonel Flack, sometimes known as "Pop" to his students. When the subject turned to tennis, his eyes lit up as he described the competition he faced in college and in the service. He regaled me with stories of tournaments, matches with famous players, games played at officers' clubs in remote parts of the world. He said, "Tennis is one game that, once you learn it, you will be able to play the rest of your life. When your knees go out and you can't play football, when there's no gang of boys around for a pickup game of basketball or baseball, you can always find someone to play tennis with." So, he convinced me. Or, perhaps it was his enthusiasm, my love for his stories and respect for his retired rank, his war experiences, or his genial personality, that I just felt I didn't want to disappoint. However it was, we agreed.

He loaned me one of his wooden rackets in its complicated screw-down press and the following day, right after early Mass on Sunday morning, he began teaching me the basics. In between suggestions about how to hold the racket and how to volley, he lectured me on the history of the sport, showed me how to score, how to adjust the net, how to anticipate the ball, how to refrain from cussing or displaying untoward emotional behavior. I think he probably bought me my first set of tennis whites that summer as well, although for the first few games I'm sure I played in T-shirt and Levi cutoffs much to his distaste. That July was my thirteenth birthday and my father bought me my own racket, a Bancroft wood, expensive, highly polished and tightly strung with catgut and protected in a standard wooden press with butterfly screws. The racket would be re-strung many times over the four years that I owned it. I would play with it in local matches, city tournaments, and even one memorable morning at the Newport Casino—where I got to volley with Poncho Gonzalez on the grass center court, courtesy of my father who owned the business next door and had persuaded the famous champion to trade a few strokes with his son.

The Colonel was, I suppose in his mid-fifties, which seemed ancient to me then. I could not imagine, as I improved my tennis skills, and learned to volley deep, hit cross-court passing shots and top-spin lobs, that he could be able to keep up with me. Surely, the student would outplay the master any day now. But it never happened.

"Pop" Flack had a whole repertoire of moves: drop shots, slices, topspin backhands, corkscrew serves, and high-bouncing serves which just cut the end of the line. He knew the angles and the limits of the court and, comfortable with these absorbed geometries, kept his young opponent racing from the net to the baseline, ragged and breathless.

As the summer passed, I improved: the muscles on my right forearm grew oversized, my lung capacity deepened, and my strokes improved from the gradual anticipation of the slides and twists the ball would take as it came off the Colonel's racket. My service improved as well, so that I sometimes caught him wrong-footed and could come to the net quickly and put the ball away. I still didn't win a set, but the games were closer and I noticed the Colonel was flushed and winded more and more often.

We played less the following year as I found new and younger competition among military dependants, boys from De La Salle Academy, and returning college players. I was often on the courts for hours each evening and on the weekends. With only two courts to play on, one had to win to keep the court and I was often a winner. Sometimes I would generously concede to play mixed doubles with couples who were waiting patiently on the sidelines.

Then one afternoon, shortly after my fourteenth birthday, all of that changed. A new boy appeared on the block: redheaded, cocky, with an easy confidence and grace and a powerful serve which could knock a poorly-gripped racket clear out of your hand. Tommy Gallagher was a compact, good-looking Irish boy who appeared from nowhere and had all the natural moves of a champion. I was blown off the court again and again in swift, blurred games of intense ferocity. I began to learn the difference between a "club player" as opposed to a "show player" or competitive athlete. Tommy played like he was born to it. There was nothing you could hit to him that he could not return. When I tried to play his game he beat me ruthlessly, contemptuously, as if I was wasting his time.

On one of these occasions, the semi-finals of a city-wide tournament, Colonel Flack was in the audience. Shamed by my 6-1, 6-0 defeat, I did not look him in the eye as I retreated back to the bench. "I'm not going to try and console you, Mike," he said. "You got sent to hell and back by that lad. And if you play him again, he'll beat you again. He's one of those kids who are a natural. But don't let him take away your pleasure in the game; don't let him do that to you. You're a club player and a decent one. Play your own game, take the shots you can, don't get caught up in his game. And don't be intimidated."

I was to play Tommy Gallagher several times over the next two years. He beat me, as he beat most of his competitors, but he won less easily as time went by, and never with the contemptuous indifference that I had felt in that one semi-final. More importantly, losing to him did not take away my love of the game or my sense of myself as a player. Partly this was true because Colonel Flack and I returned to our early morning volleys interspersed with lessons. But now the lessons had more to do with eliminating distractions, watching the ball, and feeling the sun, the sweat on my skin, the slight breeze from the ocean, hearing the thwack of the perfectly hit ball coming off the strings. He taught me to be totally present in the moment, totally aware, totally focused.

He also trained me to go after every ball regardless of whether it seemed returnable or not. He taught me to play according to my skill level, placing shots, not over-hitting because of a desire to put it away like a pro, but stroking with the steady grace and pressure of a good club player who often tires out his more ambitious, more aggressive opponents.

Finally, he taught me that graciousness is what saves the game from savagery and ugliness. He counseled me not to give in to the temptation to call a ball out when it was in, to always give the opponent the benefit of the doubt, and that it was better to lose than to win unfairly. He reminded me to hold my temper in check, to always be polite, to return the balls in a single bounce to the server when there was no one to fetch balls.

But what he couldn't teach me, and what I learned for myself over the years, was that all of this was a gift. Tennis would change with the Australian 100 mph serves of Rod Laver, the aluminum and titanium rackets, the oversized head rackets, with Wilson and Addis logos covering every piece of equipment and raiment. Bad boys like Jack McEnroe would cuss out line judges and umpires, as aggressiveness had its day and then subsided...though never completely. Competitive tennis would be enshrined in every high school and university; tennis camps would groom a new generation of players like Pete Sampras and Andre Agassi intent on making millions as they made their mark in the sport. Still, I would go right on playing my 3.5 club level game. I would play tennis in the dry heat of the Sonoran desert and on the mile-high courts of Denver; I would play in Argentina and Panama. I would play after clearing the debris off a hurricane-littered court in Florida; I would hit the low-bounce ball while bundled in a jacket in up-state New York after sweeping off the snow-covered court, and—year after year—I would sweat through grueling sets in the tropical heat of May in Guadalajara. I would play through days of political unrest and assassination in my twenties, through the bitterness of a rancorous divorce in my thirties, through the crushing death of a beloved child in my forties, then through the uncertain days of financial disasters and overseas currency devaluations in my fifties.

Now here I am in my sixties, older now than "Pop" Flack was on that summer morning when he took a skinny twelve-year old out to the concrete courts of a seaside town to give him the gift of lifelong victory. He gave me not only a way of maintaining both physical and psychological fitness, but also a way of moving with grace and a sure sense of gratitude. One of those ineffable spiritual gifts which continues to give again and again when I walk onto a sun-drenched court, go over to measure the net with my stick (a Wilson H-26 titanium racket), and all the world narrows down to the clear geometries of the white lines, to the sound of the thwock as the ball hits the strings, as my muscles respond again in their dependable way to the known rhythms of the game, and everything is suddenly whole and perfect, and the world completely intelligible.

GROWING UP CATHOLIC

MOST MEMOIRS CONTAINING A chapter with this title are certain to describe the first person narrator as sensitive and aware, discovering the absurdities in the hierarchical Church with its repressive morality, its absurd doctrinal "truths," and its myriad contradictions. Ignoring for a moment my sensitivity to mistruth and unearned authority, it was apparent to me at age thirteen that there were several articles of faith that were patently absurd.

For example:

1. The "virginity of Mary" who had a child which was allegedly "conceived by the Holy Spirit" (a succubus) while she was married to Joseph with whom she did not have sex. Joseph, of course, was both angered and confused by this until an angel told him that it was okay. Yeah, right.

2. "The transubstantiation of the Host." This was the belief that when the priest blessed the wafer of bread (host or communion) and the wine in which it was dipped, these two items literally, not figuratively, became the body and blood of Christ. Thus, Holy Communion was literally eating Jesus' flesh and draining his blood. No wonder it was hard to swallow.

3. "The Resurrection of Christ." This was called the foundation of Christian belief. It stated essentially that

after Jesus was whipped, had thorns smashed into his skull, was nailed to the cross, had a spear thrust into his side, and was left on the cross until he stopped breathing, then, clearly dead, was laid in a tomb. He managed somehow to extricate himself three days later after pushing back an enormous stone which blocked the site. Then, he appeared to his followers, not bedraggled and bloody but alert, cleaned-up, articulate and in a good sense of humor—even exchanging witticisms with Tomas and Peter.

His exchange with Peter, in fact, was one of the most interesting, humorous and Christian moments transcribed in the New Testament. Simon, henceforth to be known as Peter (the "rock" on which the Church is to be built) had denied Christ three times after Jesus' arrest in the Garden of Gethsemane. This, Jesus had predicted earlier, saying that Peter would deny him thrice before "the cock crowed," that is, by dawn the following day. As predicted, Simon Peter *did* deny all knowledge of his friend and teacher when the Roman soldiers asked him, not once but three times, also as predicted.

Now, newly risen from the dead, Jesus approaches his fickle friend and says: "Simon Peter, lovest thou me?" And Peter says, "Yea, Lord. You know I love thee." And Jesus says, "Feed my sheep." Then a second time, Jesus asks, "Simon Peter, lovest thou me?" And Simon says, "Yes, Lord, you know I love thee." And Jesus says, "Feed my sheep." Then a third time, Jesus asks, "Simon Peter, lovest thou me?" And Peter says, "Yea, truly, Lord, I love thee." And Jesus says, "Feed my lambs."

Now this is a delightful and credible story. It's something a man who believes in forgiveness might actually do after the proper acknowledgement of guilt had been offered. Peter denied Him three times; Jesus gave him an opportunity to affirm Him three times. It's all there: humor, a demand for justice, the psychological drama of contrition without groveling; absolution without a demeaning demand for a specific confession. It is about forgiving a friend, but not letting him off the hook until he had clearly seen the mechanism by which absolution comes to be granted.

This type of narrative was precisely the sticking point for my efforts to dismiss Catholicism as simply a hierarchical Church with a bundle of unpalatable doctrines and repressive rules. So many of the stories told about Jesus and the ones he told about himself had the ring of authenticity to me. Moreover, his anti-authoritarian stance, reducing the Ten Commandments to two ("Love the Lord thy God and love thy neighbor as thyself"), confronting the hypocrites of his day in the Temple, his commitment to the poor and disenfranchised (including prostitutes and thieves), seemed not only heroic but believable. Here was a person who had turned traditional morality on its head. In place of self-interest and greed, we had the rich man who had no more chance of inheriting the Kingdom of God than a camel did of passing through the eye of a needle. Instead of smacking kids around (common not only in Catholic school but in most schools of my childhood), here was a teacher who said that anyone who did this would be better off having an anvil tied around his neck and being cast into the ocean. He cursed fig trees when they had no fruit for him when he was hungry; he talked in riddles; he told stories that had ambiguous meanings; he believed in forgiving seventy times seven times; he believed in sharing what one had with those who had less (Sermon on the Mount); he believed in visiting those in prison, and not spending too much time indulging in grief.

But there was no clear method of separating the wheat from the chaff and no independent-thinking student was encouraged to do so by the priest or the nuns. You either accepted the whole package or you were a non-believer.

To reject the whole package based on central doctrinal absurdities was certainly an option, and as we grew into teenagers and went off to college many opted for just that choice. For me it was not that easy because I knew (besides my instinctive feel for what was authentic in narrative) that there were certain things in Catholicism which were psychologically sound. Although many years would pass before I would read William James and understand *The Varieties of Religious Experience,* I knew a few things, both instinctively and from experience that worked for me pragmatically. For example, I learned that forgiveness freed me from anger, resentment, preoccupation with the offenses of others, and that it gave me more creative and mental freedom. I found that letting go of anxiety and worry, and trusting in a higher source of energy ("Thy will be done") was liberating and provided me with genuine vigor. Forgiveness worked. Prayer worked, as long as it was about acceptance and not self-will.

Next, there were certain communal rituals of the Church which also had value. The elaborate requiem Mass did help transform grief into something more manageable, a shared experience, replacing the isolation of loss with a communal solidarity. Besides funerals, there was the May Procession, Benediction, the Stations of the Cross, each with its own rituals, its antiphons, its hymns, customs, incense and melodious Latin which transformed me from a skinny isolated bundle of confused and contradictory impulses into a unified being who was capable of transcendence, not in spite of the congregation, but because of it and within its naturally circumscribed boundaries that both defined and transfigured ordinary experience. Nothing in my pre-teen and teenage years as a Catholic shines more brightly than these memories.

May Procession

My father, my grandfather, and all his friends were members of the National Association of Gardeners. They had access to the finest flowers, plants and floral arrangements available. This included not only the species available in the New England growing seasons but also those from greenhouses such as tropical plants, orchids of a dozen varieties, grapes and cacti, tubers and oranges, all grown for their rich clients on the Newport estates. On May 1st, celebrated in every country except the United States as the day of worker solidarity, all of these men gathered together the best and most elaborate and rare arrangements of fruits and flowers and plants to decorate the church for the arrival of spring and to commemorate "Mary, Queen of the May." It was a celebration easily traceable to pre-Christian fertility rites with deep roots (although unexplored and likely unknown by most) in our Celtic race and animist Druidic precursors.

Boys all dressed in white suits with white carnations and a green sprigs in their lapels, lined up on the side streets near St. Augustine's Church. Girls in white communion dresses, white stockings and white shoes, all holding elaborate bouquets and with floral wreaths on their heads, formed groups behind the large green banners of the Holy Rosary Society, the blue banners of the Sodality of Mary, the martial splendor of the Knights of Columbus in their medieval military garb which included sabers. In front, the monsignor, accompanied by priests and acolytes, led the procession which wound around the Church exterior, up Marchant Street to Harrison then left onto Carroll Avenue, then past the statue of Saint Augustine, up the marble steps, facing the central carved reliefs of the oaken doors of the church. There was just a hint of spring in the air as we paraded past the banks of melting snow from the never-to-be-forgotten winter. All the while, traffic was stopped, crowds of families and well-wishers stood breathless in the spring sunlight as we passed singing in sweet melodious voices:

Bring flow'rs of the fairest, bring flow'rs of the rarest
From garden and woodland and hillside and vale;
Our full hearts are swelling, our glad voices telling
The praise of the loveliest Rose of the Vale.

O Mary! we crown thee with blossoms today
Queen of the Angels, Queen of the May.
O Mary, we crown thee with blossoms today
Queen of the Angels, Queen of the May.

For a thirteen year old boy watching the 8th grade girls ahead of me, it was impossible to look at the red highlights of Mary Sheekey's hair, the bridge of freckles across Mary Newbury's nose, or the black shine of Ana Natalini's mane against her white blouse and not associate them both with the special lushness of the day and the up-rushing of blood that, like the jonquils putting forth their first green spears, spoke of new life, sensual awakening, beauty and sex.

May Day, I know now, was synchronization by early Christians with the ancient fertility rites of the older religions it had supplanted. The gold cross replaced the phallus of the maypole; the Catholic schoolgirls stood in for the vestal virgins. But what, I ask, is wrong with that? The impulse to rejoice in the light after a season of darkness, to luxuriate in florescence after a season of frozen ground, chant joyful hymns in place of the funeral dirges for those lost in winter storms, and to celebrate the blossoming of our own neighborhood girls into teenage beauties—well, all of it was worth singing about.

There were more hymns in front of the flower-laden main altar, then the most beautiful and blondest of the junior high girls ("the one most likely to look like Mary when she matures" was the criteria for the selection as I recently read in the *Nuns' Handbook* provided by the Sisters of Mercy) placed a crown of flowers on the statue of the Virgin Mary in the side chapel. This was followed by a rosary of the Joyful Mysteries on which we meditated as we dutifully repeated the ten Hail Marys for each one: The Annunciation, The Visitation. The Nativity, The Presentation, The Finding of Jesus in the Temple. Then we marched a bit less formally from the church to a cacophony of bells and a blizzard of thrown rose pedals, waving at relatives and friends. From there we returned to our front yards and gardens for the exceptional, once-a-year afternoon of photos and ice cream, and proud uncles and discerning aunts recounting how beautiful or handsome we were in the procession. Nor were they mistaken. There was something in the light of that special day, in the music and the strewn flowers, and something that shone in our eyes on the threshold of sexual ambiguity with remnants of innocence still flickering that made us both beautiful and extraordinary.

The Way of the Cross

One of the rituals I most enjoyed as an altar boy was the Way of the Cross (*Via Crucis*), or the Stations of the Cross as they were sometimes known. This practice was developed during the Crusades when knights and pilgrims began to follow the route of Christ's way to Calvary in commemoration of his death. The devotion spread throughout Europe where, promulgated by the Franciscans as a teaching tool, it was moved inside to the churches. The popularity of the *Via Crucis* inspired some of the greatest examples of Christian art, and the medieval morality plays—essentially tableau of Christ's life—developed from the sculptured representations of the Station of the Cross in great churches and cathedral.

The *Via Crucis* is a singularly dramatic, intense and richly symbolic expression of the devotion which is at the heart of Christian belief. It is also uniquely participatory in that the individual (or the congregation) literally follows a series of fourteen "stations" represented by seven wood carvings on each side of the churches interior wall which represent the events that followed from the time Jesus was condemned to death, through his journey through the streets to Golgotha, to his death on the cross and his removal to the sepulcher.

There is a candelabrum with fifteen candles carried by one acolyte and a bell-shaped snuffer held by another. The priest bears a large and heavy bronze crucifix which he sets down heavily at each sculptured representation. They all stop, as the priest announces the station: "Jesus is condemned to death." They genuflect (*Flectamus genua. Levate.*) and the priest intones: "We adore Thee, O Christ, and we bless Thee." The congregation responds: "Because by Thy holy cross Thou hast redeemed the world."

Then a verse from the *Stabat Mater*, is sung:

Stabat mater dolorosa
Juxta Crucem lacrimosa
Dum pendebat Filius.

At the cross her station keeping
Stood the mournful mother weeping
Close to Jesus at the last.

After each of the fourteen stations the acolyte put out one of the candles until there is only one left. Then, when the last station is prayed, the candle in the center is extinguished and, with the whole church is in darkness, the priest intones: "Christ was the light of the world. And when he died, the Light was gone from the world." Then the candle is re-lighted and the congregation joins in sings: "Holy God, we praise Thy name. Lord in Heaven above, we adore thee. Infinite Thy vast domain, everlasting is Thy name."

In between the prayers and the verses of the Stabat Mater, there is a meditation on each station. I remember most vividly the one that accompanied the nailing of Jesus to the cross. It was a simple one but effective. It went something like this: "It hurts me only to prick my finger with a pin. How much more those nails must have hurt You." It was a verbal reminder which accompanied the physical discomfort of kneeling on the cold stone floor. (While the priest and the congregation merely genuflected, we altar boys had to remain kneeling.) The church was usually cold and dark. The time was late afternoon before dinner and we were hungry. But this was Lent, the ninety-day period leading up to Easter, and we were supposed to experience deprivation, discomfort, in order to be reminded of what Christ had suffered to redeem our sins.

I think we were the better for it. The psychologist and educator, William James, counsels us to do at least one uncomfortable thing each day so that we will be ready for the day when our resources are sorely taxed and we are required to persist with an important task. The experience of Lent, the wearisome task of following the Stations of the Cross, the cold, the darkness, the hunger, are to my mind much the same as the early education of the Stoics who were taught (with far less beautiful rituals) to endure the hard times that life was sure to send their way. In addition, we were taught, not simply to endure them, but to "offer them up," in gratitude for the gift of life, and to bear them without sniveling.

Benediction

Ken Follet in his *Pillars of the Earth*, a wonderful book about the building of cathedrals, unfortunately refers several times to the "unintelligible Latin of the prayers and the hymns" in the Middle Ages. My guess is that the Latin was perfectly intelligible to a large group of people, not only priests but to educated laymen, altar boys, and true devotees. It was even more so once printed missals appeared in the 16th century, of course, and easy to follow in the bilingual editions of the 1950s.

Benediction was the liturgical service of exposition and adoration of the Blessed Sacrament which concluded with a blessing (from the Latin *benedictio*) of the people. It began with the Blessed Sacrament being brought to the altar by the priest and displaced in a monstrance (from the Latin *monstrare*, to show) which consisted of a ciborium or glass holder for the host, encased in gold or silver, with gold spokes (corona) spreading out from it like a metallic sun. The priest was accompanied by two altar boys, one called a *thurifer* for the incense burner (*thurifer*) he carried on a chain, while the other acolyte had chimes or bells by his side on the steps of the altar.

The choir and the congregation sang one of the most beautiful Latin hymns ever written, while this entrance and exposition of the Blessed Sacrament was taking place. It was called the *Tantum Ergo*.

Tantum ergo sacramentum
Veneremur cernui
Et antiquum documentum
Novo cedat ritui
Preastat fides suplementum
Sensuum defectui.

The congregation was down on its knees, as the Latin hymn indicated, when the priest rose, incensed the sacrament three times, the acolyte rang his bells three times, and the rich smell of oriental spices filled the air. Then the priest put on a humeral veil, raised the monstrance, and made the sign of the cross over the people.

When this was done, the priest began to intone the Litany of the Saints, which is repetitious but beautiful in Latin, and the congregation gave the responses, also in Latin. It involved the invocation of the Father, the Son and the Holy Spirit, the Blessed Mother, and all the saints by name, such as

Sancti Michaelis Archangeli. Ora pro nobis.
Sancte Gabrielis. Ora pro nobis.
Omnes sancti Apostoli et Evangelistae. Orate pro nobis.

The litany reverberated, reminding us of the communion of saints who filled up the church calendars of our days, but it also taught us subtly the plural forms of verbs and nouns, should we be linguistically inclined. If

71

not, it still provided us with one of the oldest delights of music: that of the choral antiphony.

The service ended with the *Pater Noster* (Our Father) and a full-throated rendition of a Latin hymn, usually a version of *Te Adoremus* (We adore Thee), or *Te Guadeamus* (We praise Thee) as in "Holy God, we praise Thy name. All in heaven above adore Thee. Infinite Thy vast domain. Everlasting is Thy name."

I can only hint at the beauty, the pageantry, the symbolism, the awesomeness of the music, the poetry of the Latin, the smell of the incense, the melting beeswax of the candles, the all-encompassing sense of presence and otherness that this service brought to me. The decision to use the vernacular in church services was made a few years later by the Vatican Council, with the intent of making the services more accessible, replacing Ken Follet's "unintelligible Latin" with the banality of the local dialect. This decision also had the effect of removing much of the mystery which surrounded the profound commemoration of the Holy Sacrament which at its deepest is ineffable, and felt--not through accessible language--but through a direct experience which overwhelms the senses. The mystery of transubstantiation is at the core of Christianity, and that can never be simplified. It can, however, be made mundane and trivialized by some of the "barbaric yawps" (Whitman's phrase) of various contemporary idioms.

For those of us who listened to the hymns of the Middle Ages, who have heard the antiphonal Gregorian chant in ancient cathedrals, the tradition and universality of the Church was reaffirmed again and again by the experiences I've shared here. The generations which have followed mine have been deprived of this and, with it, the majesty, solemnity, historical connection, catholicity and grace notes of the Catholic Church. No wonder the churches have emptied and young people have turned to their CD players and DVDs. So much has been lost, not least of which was the sheer beauty and spiritual intensity of a service sung in Latin, which throughout history inspired the world's best composers and musicians.

If you have heard some of the poor translations of the hymns, and—often worse—the new versions of the Gloria or the Kyrie in English, and observed how 10% percent of the congregation is singing off-key and the other 90% not singing at all, then you would feel as I do: the sadness of a parishioner who once heard his church echo with several hundred voices praising their Lord.

The poetry of the Latin hymns and the beauty of the Greek and Latin responses with their rhythmical cadences has been lost. Think of the Stations of the Cross with *Flectamus genua. Levate*, now replaced with "Kneel down. Get up." Horrible.

The universality of the Church suffers as well from Masses said only in the vernacular. When I was a child I was told that somewhere in the world the same Mass was being celebrated every hour of the day and that, when I was an adult, no matter where I traveled I would be at home in my Church—anywhere it the world. It was catholic (universal) with a global language. Now I am older and travel a great deal, and I am a stranger in my Church. Instead of the Latin which would envelope me in the solidarity and catholicity of my religion, there are the raucous sounds of the marketplace and the street. I know there is a movement now to bring the Latin back, although it is pretty much left to the discretion of the individual priests, many of whom are too young to remember (but perhaps not too young to honor) the past. What a joy it would be to know, that someday in the not-so-distant future, from Boston to Bangladesh, from Chicago to Cairo, congregations once more might intone in one universal voice, *Credo In Unum Deum.*

The language of the Holy Roman Catholic Church should not be the language of commerce and cinema. It should be an elevated and changeless language. Often the idiomatic language has nuances which are odd or humorous and not at all proper for the house of God. And even when such unfortunate occurrences are rare, the vernacular seldom enkindles the sense of awe, or the majesty, or even the sanctity which is in keeping with the Holy Sacrifice of the Mass.

Let us bring back the poetry, the solemnity, the mystery and the wonder to our Church. Let us return to the universality (the catholicity, if you will) that distinguishes this oldest of Christian faiths from the others. My guess is that it will attract more Christians than it will shut out, that it will return to the Church a good measure of the solemnity and dignity which has been lost (especially in America) in recent years, and it will help younger Catholics to reconnect with the lost traditions of their parents and grandparents.

AND THE WORD

WHEN HIS MOTHER'S VOICE woke him at five o'clock, Michael swung his feet out from under the covers and placed them tentatively on the hardwood floor. He dressed quickly in his blue slacks, white shirt and blue blazer, the uniform of St. Augustine's.

Downstairs it was quiet except for the ticking of the hall clock. He paused briefly in the kitchen and considered having a glass of milk. Then he remembered that milk was considered a food and was not permitted before Communion. He checked his father's pack of Camels on the kitchen table; almost a full pack. He picked it up and carefully removed two cigarettes. He grabbed a few wooden matches from the stove and went out the back door, locking it behind him.

It was 5:15 and Michael was headed down the street to St. Augustine's Church only a block from his house. He was thirteen years old and the head altar boy. This meant, among other things, that he had his choice of Masses to serve. He chose to serve an early weekday Mass four to five times a month as an example to the younger boys. And while two altar boys were usually assigned to each Mass, Michael refused any partners.

The early Masses went by quickly, and the priests preferred him to serve alone. The young assistants liked him because his responses were quick and clearly articulated.

The pastor enjoyed him because his Latin was flawless and memorized. He did not have to read off the altar card which contained the end of the priest's Latin printed as a cue, and the altar boy's responses in large capitals.

Michael lit a cigarette as soon as he was around the corner from his house. He walked slowly, thinking about the Mass and about how he would like to be a priest some day himself. He had already memorized most of the prayers said by the priest at Mass. He knew how to give absolution.

This morning he was practicing the Last Gospel as he walked. It was his favorite. He rolled the words off his tongue in a deep brogue imitation of Father O'Malley as he walked.

In principio erat verbum, et verbum erat apud Deum, he rumbled, passing the privet hedge of Mrs. Fogarty's house with the flower garden beyond. He walked under the huge maples and elms which formed a dark tunnel down to the church. He felt the drippings on his jacket and the helicopter seeds of maples under his feet. Sparrows flitted in and out of the thick branches as the sun began slowly to melt the morning mist.

He passed the Sullivan sisters' house and quickly cupped the cigarette in his hand when he thought he had seen a movement at their kitchen window. He recovered his poise quickly and smiled, imagining himself a priest already, respected by the old people of the parish and admired by those watching him now from behind kitchen curtains as he made his way to the church.

"Why there goes young Father Dillon," one would say. "Isn't he the dedicated one? Up every morning, letting the others sleep in."

"Sure, he's a fine cut of a priest," the other would say. "He'll be a monsignor or a bishop before he's thirty."

He entered the old churchyard, flicked his cigarette into a rhododendron shrub by the side entrance, and opened the heavy, polished door. Inside, it was dark and redolent with odors of old wood, lemon polish, candle wax and incense. He walked down the dimly-lit hallway and opened the vestry door.

"Good morning, Sister Mary Carmel," he greeted the nun setting out the priest's vestments. He could tell from the richness of the gold brocade, the fine linen and, of course, the gem-encrusted chalice, that it was the pastor who would be saying the morning Mass.

The other priests had very simple vestments and plain sterling silver chalices with the thin gold lining for the Holy Eucharist. But Father O'Malley, whose family owned O'Malley Lumber, Inc. had a chasuble of gold and silver thread, interwoven with mother-of-pearl and semi-precious stones. His alb was made out of the finest Irish linen.

"I see it's Father O'Malley this morning, Sister," Michael remarked.

"Himself, it is. Even Solomon is his glory was never arrayed like him," the nun remarked dryly.

She had arranged the vestments in the order in which the priest would put them on: cassock, alb, surplice, the ornate chasuble of green and gold, maniple, and the black, three-cornered biretta. Now she turned her head to Michael, cocking it quizzically.

"And would ye be doin' the honor of dressin' His Reverence today, Michael?"

It was not the usual procedure, but he knew that the priest and the nun grated on each other and that he would be doing both a favor if he took over what was properly the nun's duty.

"Sure, Sister; I don't mind," he said.

"And don't I know that," she snapped. "Yer two of a kind up there on the altar. One would think that it was an Elizabethan play instead of the Lord's Holy Sacrifice, and the two of ye bellowin' Latin back and forth at each other loud enough to wake all the Protestants in Belfast. And him dressed like King Henry himself and you, the young Prince Hal."

Michael blushed and considered replying but the nun walked out before he could answer.

He went over to the acolyte's lockers and removed the black cassock from the first cubicle. He hung up the school blazer and then put on the cassock, buttoning it from the neck to the ankles. He straightened up, and then loosened the uncomfortable collar.

Dies irae, dies illa! Salvet seculum in favilla! sang a loud baritone voice outside the sacristy. "Dum-da-dum-da, Dum-da-de-dum!" And the door opened.

"The Reverend Francis Xavier O'Malley. Priest of God forever by the Order of Melchizedek. And is it the young Dillon of the County Kerry clan who will be serving with me today?" asked the priest, sticking his head in the door.

"It is, Father," the boy smiled.

"Well, then," said the priest, walking in and finally closing the door behind him. "In that case, I suppose you'll do. The poor lads from Cork are so gloomy, you know. Wouldn't do to have one of them offering up this paean of joy with an O'Malley!"

The priest was tall and heavy-set. His black suit was expensively cut, his gray hair stylish, and his freshly-shaved face was ruddy and self-assured. His blue eyes sparkled with childlike good humor.

"So, Sister Mary Fussbudget left in the nick of time, did she?"

"Yes, Father," Michael said. "She asked that I help dress you this morning."

"She did, did she? Well, it's only a parish priest you have here, not His Holiness. You just give me a hand with the chasuble at the end, Bucko, and I should be able to manage the rest.

"Yes, Father."

"Now go fill the cruets, and *cold* water, please. It's bad enough to mix any water with wine, but if it must be done, let's make it cold." Michael walked over to the cupboard and removed the gallon jug of Christian Brothers' wine. He took a funnel and first filled a quart bottle, then filled the cruet from that, then put the glass stopper in. He ran water in the sink until it was quite cold, filling the companion cruet. He placed them both on a cut-glass tray, draped a finger-towel over his arm, and arranged the cruets on a small coffee table at the side of the main altar. Then he took one of the kitchen matches out of his pocket, walked up the marble steps of the altar, genuflected, and lit the two candles on either side of the tabernacle. He bowed from the waist and walked down the front, red-carpeted stairs of the altar looking out at the handful of elderly parishioners who had trickled into the church.

He went to his locker in the vestry and got out a starched and pleated white surplice and put it on over his head. He straightened it in the full-length mirror next to the table with the priest's vestments.

Father O'Malley stood next to him, tucking his alb under the cincture, frowning at the boy as he did so.

"You should have a bit of lace on that surplice," he said. The priest's alb of pure white linen was trimmed at the hem and sleeves with four inches of intricate lace.

"Surely your father makes enough money, lad?"

"I suppose he does, Father. But my mother thinks that we spend too much as it is."

"That's where your mother's wrong, Bucko, and good Sister Mary Prisspants as well. We should present the finest version of ourselves as possible to Christ the king."

"Yes, Father."

Satisfied, the priest turned to the dressing table. Michael helped him into the green brocade chasuble with the gold-embroidered "IHS" on the back. Father O'Malley pinned and adjusted his maniple, then picked up the three-cornered biretta and placed it on his head. He put a flat linen cover over the chalice, then turned around and faced the boy. Michael put both his hands together and bowed to the priest.

"*Introibo ad altare Dei!*" boomed the priest in a clear, rich brogue when they reached the altar.

"*Ad Deum qui laetificat joventutem meam,*" Michael answered in an equally clear young voice.

"I go to the altar of God/To God who givest joy to my youth," were the words of the psalm. And here at this altar festooned with rich vases of gladioli, the covered tabernacle glowing in the light of the candles, the women echoing the responses behind him, and the priest stately above him like a true high priest before the altar, Michael felt the truth of those words.

As the Mass progressed, Michael's movements grew more fluid and the Latin spilled melodiously off his tongue. The cut-glass crystal pinged musically as he attended to the Lavabo. He rang the chimes at his side vigorously at the moment when the priest changed the bread into the Body of Christ and the wine into His Blood.

At the end, the priest turned away from the altar and blessed the congregation. He held out his hands as Michael had seen Christ do in the painting when he spoke to his disciples. *"Dominus vobiscum."* And then, *"Ite, missa est."* And Michael's *"Deo gracias"* was echoed by the tiny congregation.

When the priest came down from the altar, Michael retrieved the biretta and then held the edge of the priest's alb as together they genuflected. And Michael was filled with goodness and more than a little pride as they both rose in unison, and he followed the priest through the double door of the sacristy.

Those feelings had not diminished by the time he got home. The sun was up now and a robin was tugging fiercely at a worm as Michael walked up the front lawn to his house. He went into the kitchen and sat down to breakfast. His mother had already had a pot of oatmeal prepared. She put a bowl in front of him. It was glutinous and unappetizing.

"Well, what's the matter with you," she asked.

"Nothing," Michael said.

"Oatmeal not good enough for you, I suppose."

"Father O'Malley said that most people feed their horses what shanty Irish eat for breakfast," Michael said.

"Oh, did he now? Well, he has a cook to fry him up bacon and doughboys every morning. And a housekeeper to clean the grease, and fill his pipe, and God knows what else. He ought to keep his mouth out of other people's poor fare."

"Someday I'm going to be a priest too."

"If you are, you'll be grateful for a good breakfast of oatmeal before you start your day. Who do you think makes a priest anyway, Michael? Who do you think pays for the seminary? The priest's family, that's who. The parish gives him a small salary to live on after he's ordained, but the fine foods and nice clothes that Father O'Malley has, well—they come from his very wealthy family."

"Is that really true," I asked with astonishment.

"It is. And your father's small shop makes little enough profit for you to go to the seminary. We'd still have to borrow a bit for the university, maybe mortgage the house...."

Michael buttered his toast and took a bite. This was new information for sure. He looked at the oatmeal. It had cooled off and congealed. He pushed it away. He looked at the kitchen: old icebox, four burner gas stove, faded linoleum floor, cracked enamel on the sink. He had been feeling so wonderful just a moment ago and now...."

"You're not going to eat your oatmeal?"

"No, I'm not hungry."

"It's those darn cigarettes, isn't it? Some altar boy! Stealing your father's cigarettes. Oh, Mister Holier-Than-Thou. Too good for oatmeal. You're probably into the wine over at the church as well."

"I never touch the wine in the sacristy. I don't know where you got that. God! I hate the way you demean everything and turn everything upside down. I come home from church feeling so good and...and...."

"And holy and *special*. Well, welcome to the real world, Michael. It's not Christ the King and Gregorian chants and golden vestments. It's hard work and sacrifice and long days of worries and being poor and eating oatmeal just to keep going. A time will come when you'll be grateful for that small bit of oatmeal you passed up."

"I'd rather be dead."

"Don't wish it," his mother said. "That, too, will come to pass soon enough." She kissed him on the cheek. "I'm going upstairs now to dress. Try not to worry too much about the priesthood. You're young yet; don't take yourself so seriously.

Michael collected his lunch and then went into the small pantry. Well, it was gone now, the feeling of rightness and oneness with God, the feeling that he was chosen and special. She sure had ruined it. Mothers had a talent for that. He looked around the pantry. What was it he wanted? He saw a dozen preserve jars in a cardboard box. He took one, put it in his lunch bag, and then headed out the door.

He did not notice the towering elms or the birds as he walked to the church this time. He felt the warmth of the sun as a prickling of sweat beneath his shirt. He also felt angry and prematurely guilty because he had already made his decision.

Here he was in a state of grace, too. But, immediately upon thinking that, he convinced himself that what he was about to do was not actually stealing—it was payment for services rendered. After all, he had worked right along with the priest. And the priest got to drink the wine.

His thirteen year-old mind was quick as a Philadelphia lawyer's. He even reminded himself to say an Act of Contrition as soon as he had done the deed. No sense in taking chances.

When he got to the sacristy he closed the door behind him and walked directly over to the cabinet. He took the glass jar out of the paper bag and filled it from the gallon jug of altar wine. He walked over to the school and told the eighth grade teacher that he had a dental appointment. The nun excused him without suspicion.

He hurried out the side door of the school, ignoring the questions of the other students on the playground. He was going down to the waterfront where the ships from Cruiser-Destroyer Fleet Atlantic defended the deep harbor, and launches scurried among their gray hulks.

When he got there he found a secluded spot below the seawall and sat down to drink the wine. The tide was out. Seaweed and blue-black mussels gleamed on the exposed rocks, while the sun glinted on the soft waves. He drank a sip of wine and felt its warmth going down to his near-empty stomach, and then rising in a fine rush to his head. He felt free, alone and at peace.

"In principio erat verbum et verbum apud Deum!" he said aloud and laughed. The words did not seem so magical or so majestic here beside the ocean under the enormous canopy of sky. Maybe, he thought, words need to be closed in by something before they had power, like candles need to be closed in by darkness if they are to shine. A candle in the sun is a puny thing.

"Puny," he said aloud, testing the sound of the word. "PUUUNYYY!" he shouted out to the destroyers anchored in the Bay.

He lit the other cigarette which he had taken from his father's pack of Camels before Mass. Was it only this morning? It seemed like ages ago. He relished the rich smoke, the sweet taste of the wine and the feeling in his blood. He felt wise. He felt that he had learned something important this morning, although he could not say exactly what it was. But it didn't matter really. The wine, the ocean, the puny ships and the sailors on the decks—all there. And the seagulls quarreling over the exposed mussels, and the crabs scuttling sideways over the seaweed-laden rocks.

He drank the last of the wine and leaned back against the wall. He felt warm despite the sea breeze. He looked out at the sailboats tacking against the wind, their canvases snapping, white hulls gleaming, and thought that he had never seen a day so lovely.

And he knew then, suddenly and clearly, that he could always find a way to shut out the voices of skeptics and naysayers and the purveyors of an oatmeal existence; that he could always find a private place—better than any church—where he could focus on what was pure and true and beautiful, and that no one could ever take that away. And, he knew, taking another deep pull on the wine, no one ever would.

WOULD YOU SHOW IT TO JACK?

MY FATHER TRULY BELIEVED, as Bishop Fulton J. Sheen did, that "the family that prays together stays together." So each night we prayed the rosary for the "peace in the world and the conversion of Russia." We did this right after the supper dishes were washed, dried and cleared away. Some nights it seem interminable as we repeated Hail Mary after Hail Mary and until we were half brain dead with repetition. We said all five decades while kneeling on the floor so it was a double relief when we could get up, sit back on the couch and listen to my mother read.

My mother loved to recite poetry and memorized some of the classics of her day. Many a night, before the advent of television and its inevitable intrusion into our family life, we would listen for hours to her read from her well-worn *Best Loved Poems of the American People*. First published in 1936 and dedicated to the memory of Adolph S. Ochs, long-time publisher of the New York Times, by editor Hazel Felleman, this volume contained just about every kind of poem written in English. Narrative verse and doggerel stood side by side with Shelley and Byron. Mother especially liked dramatic poems such as "The Wreck of the Hesperus," "Paul Revere's Ride," "The Cremation of Sam Magee" (my Dad's favorite), Poe's classic verse, "The Raven," and the well-known Civil War poem, "Barbara Frichie."

Up from the meadow rich with corn,
Clear in the cool September more,
The clustered spires of Frederick stand
Green-walled by the hills of Maryland.
Round about them orchards creep
Apple and peach tree fruited deep
Fair as the Garden of the Lord
To the eyes of the famished rebel hoard.

So here comes the Confederate Army in 1863 marching through the streets of Fredericksberg, Maryland with conquest on their mind. They number in the thousands with artillery, rifles and cavalry. Nervous about counter-attacks and even sniping from townspeople hiding behind the curtained windows buildings which line the streets, they have orders to wipe out all resistance whether military of civilian and this includes shooting anyone who brandishes the Stars and Stripes. As they pass beneath the house of an elderly woman by the name of Barbara Frichie, she waves the American flag from her bedroom window in clear defiance of the invaders. Before a rebel trooper can get off a shot, the Confederate general shouts:

Who touches a hair of yon gray head,
Dies like a dog! March on," he said.

Quite thrilling to see both the courage of the old woman and also to observe the gallantry of the Southern general that refuses to shoot a defiant housewife who showed more courage than most of us could have imagined under the circumstances. My mother read it with gusto, with changes in inflection, with dramatic gestures and flair. My father would often take his turn as well with the reading of "Casey at the Bat" or "The Village Blacksmith." Sometimes they would read something more reflective such as Longfellow's "The Psalm of Life," Runyard Kipling's "If," or Seeger's "I Have A Rendezvous With Death," or Frost's "The Road Not Taken."

The favorite poem of my grandfather when he came to visit was one that was written by a minor poet. A contemporary of Byron, Shelley, Keats and the rest of the Romantics, little of his work is remembered today except the little poem that my grandfather memorized, "Jenny Kiss'd Me," which he loved and would recite it at the drop of a hat:

Jenny kiss'd me when we met
Jumping from the chair she sat in
Time, you thief, who loves to get
Sweets in your list, put that in!
Say I'm weary, say I'm sad
Say that health and wealth have miss'd me.
Say I'm growing old, but add
Jenny kiss'd me.

"You don't need to publish reams and reams of poems like Yeats, or dense, obscure and unreadable novels like Joyce to live forever. All you need to do with your life is write one unforgettable poem," he said.

"But nobody ever heard of this guy," I protested. "What's his name? Leigh Hunt?"

"You've heard the saying that *the story outlives the teller?*" my grandfather asked. "Well, the poem outlives the poet, and is always finer."

So, it came as no surprise to anyone that when Dylan Thomas and his obituary was published in *Time*, my mother had cut not the obit itself but the accompanying poem from the magazine and put it on the refrigerator. The lines were difficult for someone used to the easily accessible Longfellow and fascinating.

The force that through the green fuse drives the
flower
Drives my green age; that blasts the roots of trees
Is my destroyer.
And I am dumb to tell the crooked rose
My youth is bent by the same wintry fever.

Now here was something quite different. No longer the straight forward narrative of Longfellow or even gentle philosophical renderings of Frost, but a violent rendering of the life force in a tight inventive imagery. A fuse lit at birth waiting to explode and shatter life itself. I don't remember that we had any discussion regarding this poem. I think both my mother and father liked the bit about the rose since he was a gardener and an amateur botanist.

At any rate I began writing verses about that time. They were mostly derivative and mostly rhyming. I had a good sense of metrics though, so they were rhythmic and scanned well. Mostly they were either condescendingly commented on ("Very Nice, Michael.") or politely ignored. That is, until one day when I decided to write a poem about a friend of my father's with whom I had worked over the summer. His name was Jack and he was a gardener at one of the estates in Newport. He also drank a half pint of Seagram's whiskey for lunch each day in the potting shed north of the main vegetable garden. He was a decent guy and a good boss. But he was also obviously an alcoholic. I wrote what I thought was a sympathetic portrait of the gardener's lost youth and his longing. I imagine how Jack, disappointed in love, decided to drink his life away. Although the original has been lost to posterity (alas!) here is a bit that I remember.

> So there he is each noon 'mid broken pots
> Lifting bottle to hungry mouth and not
> To bring forth joy or launch a party here
> But to forget the past, outlive despair.

My father found the draft on my desk and out of curiosity (or perhaps I left it there for him to discover) read it and was immediately outraged. "This is not funny! This is not something you use your gift of writing for, to hurt and belittle other people. I am really disappointed in you, Mike."

I tried to explain that I had no intention of doing hurting or belittling anybody. It was just a poem that observed someone and speculated on his motivations. But he would have none of it. "Would you show it to Jack?" he asked me. "Do you think he would be honored that you wrote such things about him?"

I did not argue the point. Of course, I would not show it to Jack. Nor did I think he would be honored.

However, that still did not mean that the piece was not worth writing, or that the subject matter (or the subject) should be ignored. It merely meant that I needed to be more careful in the future about leaving drafts of my writing around the house. I realized that good intentions could be just as deadly to creativity as active censorship. Even those who love us the most, I realized, could eviscerate the best products of our imagination with a phrase.

PERMISSION TO SPEAK

AS A CHILD I had a terrible stammer which worsened as adolescence came with its emotional stresses and changes. I could not pronounce a vowel without a machinegun stutter of repetition. "Aa-aa-aa-apple," I would say. "Or-or-or-orange," I would splutter. In anticipation of such problems, I had learned to glue articles or adjectives to such words so that a consonant would preface each noun. "Give me th'apple," I'd say or "N"orange, please." All this planning went out the window, however, in times of emotional excitement when through enthusiasm or anger the words flowed faster than my deliberation could arrange them.

This weakness, this flaw, had its compensations at times. In the effort to find adjectives, to rearrange sentences, I developed a facility with language and a skill at rearranging words. All my comments were second draft and thus when I did finally speak, my words often had a deliberation and weight to them which they retain today. My wife remarks that I seem to invest a simple comment about taking out the garbage with all the high seriousness of a declamation on the vagaries of the Supreme Court.

Yet at the age of fourteen stammering was a painful and embarrassing infirmity. A bright child, I was often faced with the dilemma in class of not answering a question I knew for fear of making a spectacle of myself, or answering the question after taking pains in word order and placement of consonants only to find to my chagrin that there was a follow-up question I had not anticipated. Here's a typical example of the second scenario:

"Can anyone tell us who the most important Catholic philosopher was? Yes, Michael?"

"That would be the philosopher, Thomas" (watch the **A** coming up), ah Thomas S'Aquinas. He was the" (change author for) "writer who gave us *the Summa Theologica.*"

"Very good, Michael. And what was the name of the Greek philosopher who influenced him?"

"Ah, ah, eh, eh, eh, ay, aghr, Aristotle!"

I sat down to a chorus of laughs which obliterated my previous answer and relegated me to the position of class fool. Or worse: an object of pity to Mary Newbury with whom I was desperately in love. I had not told her my feelings, of course, and my chances of declaring them and being taken seriously had vanished forever after this latest exhibition.

One day, shortly after this episode, my ninth grade English teacher, Brother Felix, asked me to come see him after my last class. Our school was run by French Christian Brothers who had their rectory on school grounds. As a result, staying after school was not a hardship for the teachers. Essentially, they lived at school. Nevertheless, looking back now, except for the coaches and the most exigent of the disciplinarians, few hung around the school after the last bell.

Brother Felix was erasing the blackboard when I went in. He told me to have a seat and then he began telling me about his own school years. He told me that when he was a teenager he used to stutter but that he seldom did anymore. "How did you get over it?" I asked. He told me

93

that essentially he used two tools which were readily available: singing and projecting the voice.

"Do you like to sing?" he asked. I nodded. "And I'll bet you don't stutter when you sing, am I right?" I nodded again.

That week at his suggestion, I joined the school choir and began what would be a lifelong amateur passion for music. Even today I sing at Irish gatherings on St. Patrick's Day, I sing Christmas carol each holiday season, I sing in church, and I sing with and to my own English classes at the school where I teach. At Brother Felix's suggestion, I practiced for Glee Club recitals, I sang solos in the school's talent show, I sang high masses in the local Catholic Church, and I enriched my life in ways I could not have imagined then through my studies of choral singing, Latin and French, and the history of music.

The skills involved in projecting the voice were harder to learn. I began by shouting memorized speeches and poems to the back of the class where Brother Felix sat correcting papers, apparently indifferent to my efforts and focused on his grade book. At the end of the hour, though, he smiled, and noted how many lines I had recited without a stammer. By my sophomore year under his tutelage, I had learned gestures, dramatic pauses, voice modulation, and breathing control. I had memorized dozens of poems, speeches and scenes from plays. I had even begun to write my own scripts and short speeches. By my junior year I had won oratory contests across the state, had been on a nationally televised debate tournaments, and had given extemporaneous talks in competitions, Toastmasters, student legislatures and at the Model U.N. in New York.

I discovered that, for me, speaking to large audiences was no more stressful than answering a question in class had been, or asking Mary Newbury for a date. The former I did with greater frequency. That latter, on the occasion of our junior prom, and Mary accepted with the comment: "Why did you take so long. I liked you when we were in the 9th grade."

I discovered through this experience that focusing on a weakness with determination and diligence could turn that flaw into a strength. Speaking to my graduation class, I received applause, not laughter or embarrassed silence. Much of it was due to the intervention of a caring and dedicated teacher. Brother Felix, long since passed away, is part of who I am today. I will never forget that and I try to emulate his example through my mission as a teacher. He gave me far more than a tool for dealing with a handicap. He gave me the key to the secret of living fully.

I am still a stammerer, of course. I have simply discovered a method wherein I manage to avoid stuttering most of the time, but always the tendency is there. Michael, the 9th grade student, is forever a part of who I am. When I am sufficiently moved by the language, or by an emotion, a click ascends in the larynx that sometimes is converted into a lilt, a thoughtful pause, a Kennedyesque repetition, or a doubling of the consonant. Other times, it results in a dramatic turn in thought or image as I move to replace one word with another less trouble to the tongue.

For most of those who hear me speak, these devices are unremarked, or noticed simply as a wide range of emotional devices used by a speaker comfortable with language and ideas. Yet for Michael, the boy in the front row with his hand up, dreading what will come out of his mouth, they are the tools which make him a teacher today. For Michael, the boy in the basement declaiming Patrick Henry's "Give me liberty or give me death," the boy in the choir transcendent with music, they are and always will be the stuff of miracles.

SUMMER WORKERS

NEWPORT, RHODE ISLAND, IN the late Fifties was still a remote island cut off from the rest of the world. Access was through a series of small villages to the Jamestown docks where you waited sometimes for an hour in the summer for the boat to arrive. Then you boarded the Jamestown Ferry to cross Narragansett Bay, a forty-minute cruise past sailing ships and fishing vessels to the ferry dock on the Newport side by the local jail. The only other way of getting to the island was across Mount Hope Bridge to the west, through Tiverton and Middletown. In those days you didn't take a drive to Newport, you took a trip, or went on an excursion. All of that changed with the construction of the Newport Bridge. A once-interminable journey (we are *seriously* going to Newport) has now become a matter of a ten minute drive across the Claiborne Pell Bridge.

What's also changed is the exclusiveness of the island, the feeling of solitude, of being part of a world unto itself. Once an enclave for the super rich, along with salty sea dogs, Portuguese fisherman and Irish gardeners, the Newport of the new millennium is a condominium-filed, traffic-choked playground of moderately prosperous young executives, surrounded by mansions converted into luxury apartments, or preserved by the local historical society as costly bookmarks in the island's forgotten narrative.

In 1957 my grandfather worked as the head gardener at one of the lovely estates owned by Robert Goelet which still prospered then, despite the growing costs of labor, the high property taxes, and the changes in conspicuous consumption. Goelet was interesting because, besides owning a large chunk of Manhattan and being one of the richest men in America, his son Robert married the heir to Gardiner's Island, the only remaining unspoiled island paradise left on the eastern seaboard.

I was fourteen at the time and like most Irish boys had been working from the age of twelve each summer, cutting grass on the estate, working in the greenhouse during rainy weather, pruning tress, pushing a wheelbarrow from the potting shed to the multi-acre gardens. The gardens had everything from Lima beans to French white corn, from strawberries to melons, from gladioli to roses, and were an interminable labor. Fresh fruits and vegetables as well as cut flowers were brought daily to the "big house." My grandfather, respectfully known as the Old Man, besides supervising half a dozen men, also oversaw activities of houseboys and maids to whom he gave daily instructions. He provided jobs to local landscape contractors, and did thousands of dollars of business with seed, bulb and supply companies from Massachusetts to Holland. It's hard to picture what the island was like then. The great gardens are gone now and the land is part of Salve Regina College, a secular institution exempt from taxes.

Days working in the fields were long. There was a variety of tasks and most of them were done by hand. There were no tractors (except a borrowed one for spring plowing, and sometimes for the August baling of hay) and few power tools. The work was physically intensive and was always touted as "a good way to stay in shape" for football or hockey. These were the most common fall and winter sports played by local boys on small, but highly competitive, school teams. The work was hard but with enough variety so that boredom was not debilitating. There were the early morning tasks of feeding the poultry, collecting the eggs, watering the strawberries, and then cutting gladioli, chrysanthemums and long-stemmed roses for the floral displays at the manor breakfast table. Then there were rows of beans to hoe, tomatoes and peas to be staked-up, fields of hay to scythe. At noon we found a spot out of the sun to eat our ham sandwiches with fresh iceberg lettuce and sun-ripened tomatoes picked from the garden.

A half hour later we were back at it. Cutting the hay, raking, then binding it in sheaves. Then over to the corn fields, hoeing the late-planted crop, picking the earlier rows, followed by shucking and cleaning so that there would be plenty for the evening meal which the cooks were already beginning to prepare at the manor. When that was done there was the sweeping-up around the potting shed, feeding the poultry, sharpening the scythes and hoes, wishing for a cold beer but knowing that my grandfather, a teetotaler, would offer nothing better than a draught of well water at the end of the day or a drink from the hose when we had finished washing up.

Conversation was not encouraged during the sunny weather when there were so many chores to be done. Although, New England reticence being what it is, conversation would not have been easy to come by anyway. But when the August rains came and most of the crops had been harvested, we often retreated to the barn or the potting shed where we did light carpentry, repaired the tack and tools, and sometimes chatted. The usual form of male camaraderie in those days was a rough form of teasing. It was something I was never very good at and didn't particularly enjoy. In fact, I had grown quite accustomed to the extended silence of the working summer days. Like the Frost line, "men work together though apart," I found a comfort in being a part of a working crew, judged not by my underdeveloped fourteen year-old body or my adolescent insecurities, but solely by my abilities to do a man's work.

Both the workers and I knew that there were differences between us. Most of them had never gone to high school and I was in a Catholic prep school. I would go on to the university and be part of a profession. They were day laborers who had always worked with their hands, digging ditches, planting crops and harvesting, leased out to estate managers, farmers, landscape contractors and construction crews. My grandfather was their boss. My father owned his own business and was comfortably ensconced in the entrepreneurial middle class. If there were resentments about any of that, however, they were never articulated in the fields.

Now in the coolness of the potting shed as the men sat around smoking pipes and cigarettes or spitting tobacco juice in a can, and the Atlantic squall blew against the soil-rimmed windows, I braced myself for the ribbing which always came when older men had a youngster in their midst.

"So, Mike, me boy," said old Willie, a seventy-year-old whose teeth were yellowed with age and tobacco. "Have a smoke, sit back and relax."

"Oh, no, he dasn't dare have a smoke," said his friend, a thin dour man in his forties, balding, and with a thin-lipped County Cork smile. "He's getting in shape, you see, to play American football."

I smiled and nodded. "Thanks, anyway. No, I don't smoke."

"Well, have a chew then," said Willie, cutting off a plug of tobacco with a pocket knife and offering it. "Sure, you're a man, ain't you?"

There was never any right thing to do under circumstances like these. I think back to those rainy days, those potting-shed conflict days, as the most dreaded of my adolescence. If I took the plug of tobacco, I might get sick and embarrass myself, showing them that indeed I was not a grown man at all. If I did not take the plug, I would be shown up as either a sissy who was afraid, or a prep school brat who felt himself superior to the working class. What I did, in fact, was to take the stupid plug of tobacco, chew it, and inadvertently swallow a good portion of the juice before I had enough sense to begin spitting. I was accordingly laughed at anyway, despite showing myself to be a real man. I was unable to eat my lunch, as I remember, and had a queasy stomach for the rest of the afternoon.

Still the days drew on towards September, inexorably. The harvest of the late corn arrived, the last of the beans, followed by the plowing under of the corn stalks and the desiccated bean plants to enrich the soil, and the rains. I had still not grown used to the bull sessions in the potting shed. I prayed for good weather. Perhaps because I sensed beneath the joking the razor-edged animosity towards the boss's grandson, toward my whole generation whose only dream was to get off the island and never have to touch a hoe or a shovel again. And, perhaps, I sensed in myself contempt for these men who so transparently had let their lives drift to this point. Men who never read a book, whose only thought at the end of the day was the oblivion of a tap room, swilling down draft beer and shots of Four Roses, and complaining about the work, the weather, or their bad breaks in life.

This time, one of the younger workers led off with the teasing. His name was Charley Harkens and he was in his early twenties, an eighth grade drop-out. He was heavy in the shoulders and legs, well-built in those days before weight machines and gym memberships, when the only muscles you had were the ones you got from working hard. His biceps split the sleeves of his T-shirt and his chest was full.

"So, Mike, you're going out for football in the spring," he said with a predatory smile.

"Yeah, Charley, but just the junior varsity," I replied disconsolately.

"What position are you going to play?" he asked.

Well, frankly, I had no idea. I was only going out for football because my father and my uncle had played, because I was expected to play. And also because not to go out for football at our school relegated you to the sidelines of all the action, including girls. But I was in good shape from working in the fields, I had strong shoulders and forearms; I could run like the wind and I wasn't afraid of getting hit.

"What position?" I repeated playing for time.

"Yeah," said Charley. "You know, end, guard, fullback, quarterback."

For most of the old Irishmen listening to the conversation, it might as well have been Greek. Football to them meant something entirely different. They played rugby or soccer as schoolboys, not American football. But they caught the tone in Charley's voice and knew that there was something afoot in this line of questioning.

"Well, the way it works out is that you just show up on the first day of practice and then they have tryouts," I ventured, flying solely by the seat of my pants. "You know, to see how good you can throw the ball, how fast you can run, how good you can catch?"

"And block and tackle, right?" added Charley, with a curl to his lip.

"Well, yeah, that too, I guess." I had only played sandlot football and that was touch, not tackle. So, what I knew about blocking and tackling was rudimentary.

The rain had let up and the sun was coming out again. My grandfather appeared at the door of the shed and told the men to get their tools and get back to work.

"After work," Charley said, punching me in the arm. "After work we'll come back here and work on your blocking." He walked away and headed over to the corn fields. My grandfather put his hand on my arm.

"What was that about, son, or do I want to know?" my grandfather asked.

"Nah, nothing," I said and went to help load a truck of vegetables for the manor house. But it *was* something, of course, and it occupied my mind for the next two hours until quitting time. I crunched the gears driving the truck up to the big house, tracked mud on the cook's shiny kitchen floor and got yelled at. Out of nervousness, I even smoked one of my grandfather's cigarettes left in the glove compartment of the truck before returning it to the barn a good ten minutes after quitting time. The men were still there, all gathered around Charley.

"You're late," Charley said. "You weren't trying to avoid me, were you?"

"No, I just had some work to do for the Old Man," I lied.

"Well, said Charley, taking off his shirt and rolling his shoulders. "Get down in a three-point stance and let's see how good you are." He got down in a crouch and I followed, facing him in a classic blocking position. The men gathered around to watch.

"Willie," he called to the old man. "You yell out, one, two, three, HUT. And when he says 'HUT,' Mike, I'm going to try to get by you or *through* you; it don't make much difference. And you have to try and stop me. Got it?"

I nodded.

"One, two, three, HUT!" and an elbow ripped into my jaw and laid me out, flattened in the dust and dung-mottled floor of the barn. I got up, brushed off my pants, shook my head, and returned to the three-point stance.

"One, two, three, HUT!" and I was slammed to the ground by a shoulder to the gut.

We did it over a dozen times. Each time I landed on the ground, more battered and bruised than the last. I kept returning to the classic position. He kept slamming me into the ground. Finally he got tired and left off.

"Come on," I said. "Let's do it again. Don't quit now.

104

"Nah," Charley said, sweat beaded on his forehead. "That's enough. You've had enough for one day."

Most of the men were sheepishly looking away, getting their lunch pails, putting on their jackets, edging toward the barn door.

"One more time, you son of a bitch," I said quietly.

"What the Sam Hill is going on here!" roared my grandfather coming into the barn. "Jist a little football practice, sir," Charley meekly offered. "Jist giving the boy a few pointers."

"What in blazes do you know about football, you big galoot. Get out o' here and get back to yer cronies at the bar."

"What a minute, Grandpa," I said. "I've just about got the knack of it." It had occurred to me, after getting knocked down and battered a dozen times, that I didn't have to play Charley's game. The point after all was simply to get to the other side. I turned to my opponent. "This time, Charley, you block me, and I'll try to get around you."

Charley looked at my grandfather for permission and the old man nodded. The workers gathered around. Charley set up in a blocking position but he was awkward, cumbersome getting set up. His football prowess, as I guessed it, was merely bunk.

"One, two, three, HUT!" and—as he moved forward with his powerful shoulders—I swiveled on the balls of my feet, launched myself over his body, then ran the length of the barn carrying an imaginary football into an imaginary end zone. Charley, forced off-balance, landed face down in the dust.

My grandfather went over to him and gave him a hand up. He looked at him with a mixture of pity and contempt.

"Like I said, Charley, you don't know a damn thing about football. Stick to the fields. Now, Mike, if you're through playing around, let's go home. There's more important things to do, and your mother will likely have supper on the table."

That barn was torn down over thirty years ago. There is a lacrosse field there now, some bleachers at one end where the corn used to grow, and a pair of tennis courts at the other where beans were plowed under that August of 1957. When I passed by there last fall on one of my rare visits home, I wanted to get out of the car, get down in a three-point stance and run to the end of the field. But what would be the point? I'm already on the other side.

RADIO, REVOLUTION AND ROCK AND ROLL

"WELCOME TO WADK-AM. Fifteen-forty on your radio dial," is how I greeted everyone on a Saturday morning with my new show. Hired in my junior year by the local radio station, I broadcasted a one-hour special every Saturday with "news from around the world," sports, rock and roll and "teen happenings" in Newport, Middletown, Jamestown, Portsmouth and Tiverton. My mentor was the famous Francis John Pershing Sullivan, known more familiarly as "Sully," a colorful radio talk show host of immense popularity and genuine charisma.

He taught me everything I needed to know: how to get the news right off the teletype; how to "red-line" edit it, and then cut it in time for the "News on the Half Hour." He also showed me how to hold a 45 rpm record in the groove while I was talking or making a dedication so that the song would play immediately when I released it, without the fifteen seconds of dead airtime which failure to do so would ensure. The most important thing he taught me, though, was how to always "act as if." This meant acting as if one was always excited about the latest new product or service the advertiser provided. Acting as if one was always *up* and delighted to be bringing the news to the folks in the region and reporting the sports and sharing the latest R&B hit. Always acting as if one was angry when the Red Sox lost a game, or the Russians put up a satellite into outer space.

107

"The audience can hear the slightest non-genuine tone in your voice, Mike. So you have to train yourself to always believe that what you are saying, or what you are feeling, is true. So, whether you consider Bardahl Engine Treatment wonderful or not, just tell yourself: *It is great that they are paying my salary.* Now that's something to be excited about, right? Learn to show your emotions in your voice. No one can see your face but they can hear the emotion and the sincerity in your voice."

I had come a long way from the shy and stammering wimp in the ninth grade with the help of Brother Felix at De La Salle. Now I was a veteran public speaker, a member of a championship debate team, and the youngest person on the air in Rhode Island with his own show. It was heady stuff. And the job was not easy, especially after Sully left me on my own the second week of the job. There was the rush to get the news off the teletype and edited early Saturday morning with no one there but an engineer; the choosing of the records to play and lining them up, along with my notes of high school gossip and a list of promised dedications; then there were the local commercials to review. Local restaurants, bait shops, hair products, soft drinks and car products. There was the local news, the national news and even the international headlines.

1959 was an exciting year. Castro's revolution was in full swing and he was the hero of the hour as he defeated the evil dictator Batista and brought his troops into La Habana. Shortly thereafter he was given a ticker tape parade down Broadway in New York and the world cheered. All that would change, of course. But not right away.

Speaking of changes...It was the year the flag changed with Alaska and Hawaii both being added and the perfect arrangement of forty-eight stars being altered in what most felt was an unaesthetic way. But for most of us in those days, it was sports, girls and rock and roll which led the league in things to talk about.

"And now from the City by the Sea, going out to our good friends in Middletown, here is a little bit of Elvis from Johnny to Sandra, from Jimmy K to Alice and from the seniors at DLS to the girls at St. Catherine's. These are lonely men, girls, and what they have to say is: 'I Need your Love Tonight.'" I would play the Elvis record and in case the nuns were listening I'd follow it up with Lloyd Price, "I'm Gonna Get Married" so there would be no question of advocating sex out of wedlock which was still in those days a prohibited topic. We were on the cusp of the Sixties but it was still a mostly intolerant time. Blacks were still called Colored People or Negros and had their separate water fountains and bathrooms in the South. Schools were mostly segregated, not only in Georgia but even in South Boston.

I played lots of songs by Buddy Holly, the Big Bopper and also by seventeen-year-old Richie Valens as well. 1959 was the year all three died in a plane crash; it was later referred to in song as "the day the music died." Most of us had a special feeling for Richie Valens. He was about our age; had only a couple of hits but showed great promise. Also for those of us studying Spanish, we could practice our accents with La Bamba. "Yo no soy marinero soy capitán, soy capitán, soy capitán. "Romeo and Juliet" was our favorite play, and most of us believed that we would die young as those lovers did. Death was in the air. Lou Abbot of Abbot and Costello died; Alfalfa from the kid's show "Our Gang" was shot to death. Billy Holiday died, and the largest

109

state funeral we had witnessed in our lifetime was held for John Foster Dulles, the longtime Secretary of State. His funeral was small change, however, compared to that waiting in the wings for the future president once Eisenhower turned over the reins of power. But in 1959, Senator Kennedy was not anyone's favorite to replace him. It looked more like Stevenson and Nixon. No one yet could conceive of Catholic president.

As I reported the news in the months and weeks that followed, the candidates being considered to replace Eisenhower were Barry Goldwater, Henry Cabot Lodge and Richard Nixon for the Republicans. For the Democrats they were Hubert Humphrey and Adlai Stephenson. John F. Kennedy was running but almost everyone felt that he didn't really stand a chance. Anti-Catholic prejudice which defeated New York Governor Al Smith in his 1928 bid for the presidency was still alive and well in many states in the Union. What everyone underestimated was the political machine of the Boston Democrats, the money of Joe Kennedy, the power of televised debates, and the good looks and charisma of the young senator from Massachu-setts. Even so, it was a close thing.

One Saturday when I couldn't find the real dedication (which I had written on a slip of paper and somehow discarded, I announced: "This next song goes out to our favorite football coach. He knows who he is!" The song was "Cookie, Cookie, Lend Me Your Comb." It was about a boy so in love with himself that his girlfriend had to beg him for his comb when they were out together on a date so he would stop combing his own hair and look over at her. Our football coach at De La Salle Academy, Mr. Peterson, was known for his vanity and also for the complete absence of a

110

sense of humor. But who would have suspected that he would tune in to a kid radio announcer on a Saturday morning?

The weekend passed without incident. School was normal on Monday. That afternoon I suited up and went out on the football field. We did calisthenics and then it was time for tackling practice. The most common tackling drill consisted of running between two rows of players for about twenty yards at full speed. At the end of the row there would be a tackler. You had to drive over him if you could, or take the hit like a man if he was too big and tough for you. Then you would move into the line and wait until it was your turn to be the tackler. When I made my run, I was hit hard at the end of the tunnel by Jack Crowley, one of our biggest and meanest linemen. Dizzy and a bit sore in the ribs (we had no rib pads in those days) I went to take my turn in the ranks. "Let's try that again," Coach Peterson called out. "That wasn't much of a tackle Crowley. Let's put your shoulder into it." So, instead of taking my place in the ranks, I went to the end of the line again. I got down in a three-point stance and ran the gauntlet a full speed again. This time I was hit with such shocking force that I also lost my lunch. I went to the sideline and bent over from the waist with dry heaves. Couch Peterson came to my side. "How about you give me five laps around the field, Hogan? That should loosen you up." As I headed onto the cinder track to do my laps, he said "By the way, when you get back to the locker room, I'd be glad to lend you my comb."

I supposed I should have been flattered my show was THAT popular.

FREEBODY PARK

IN AUGUST WHEN THE Jazz Festival and the Folk Festivals were over, the grass watered, fertilized and rolled, and the cinder track around the field raked, it was time for varsity football try-outs at Freebody Park (now known as Toppa Field, after a legendary coach of the Rogers High football team).

I was a five-foot-ten, 150 pound sandlot player; my Dad had been a varsity center on the division –winning team in 1930. I had little to recommend me besides my father's past glory which was memorialized in a glass-enclosed case at the entrance to the school. I was an average runner, a poor passer, a lousy kicker. My hands were too small to be a good receiver.

My best friend from Tiverton was trying out for tackle. He was a weight-lifter who weighed 180 and was a natural athlete. The only kid skinner than me, Dave Lovejoy at 135 pounds and 5'6", was trying out for halfback, could run the 100 in under 10 seconds, was elusive, wiry and resilient. Terry Reagan, a good-looking and talented ball-handler and passer, as well as a popular student leader, was the obvious quarterback. I didn't know which position I would try out for; I was just showing up, going through the motions, and waiting to see what would happen.

The first couple of days consisted of conditioning: pushups, jumping jacks, and knee-bends, duck squats, wind sprints. Then we were issued pads and practice uniforms, followed by days of blocking, and occasional scrimmages. And then came the more challenging tackling drill in which one had to run twenty yards down the field, through a gauntlet of players, directly in the path of a tackler. I described this earlier and will not do so again. Once you had made your run, you were allowed to move to the gauntlet, and then as a tackler, and then reversed roles again.

I had done this several times and decided that I enjoyed being on the tackling end more than the running end. Unless the runner was a natural, like Clem Rego, son of a Portuguese immigrant who would be our fullback and churned his legs and twisted as he came through the line, one tended to get creamed in the exercise. Our little potential halfback was badly battered and bruised, and would have been cut from the team were it not for some amazing broken field running in a scrimmage later in the day.

For me, as the line-ups were becoming clearer, and the positions were being filled, it was apparent. If I did not want to get cut from the team, I had to choose a job that no one else wanted. Middle linebacker on defense and center at offense. I was the only contender. So, I practiced my snaps day and night. I practiced blocking at home with my Dad and at my summer job working as a landscaper. I ate and I ate and I ate, trying to gain more weight. The days went by and I studied the play book and memorized my required blocks for each play. I learned the best way to use my body to provide leverage in blocking, and how to grab the jersey of my opponent in ways which could not be detected as holding by the referees. I discovered that in defense, the knowledge of the likely plays and an ability to see telegraphed movements by the potential ball carrier would serve me in good stead as a linebacker. Still, I took a beating. I can't recall one day in the football season when I was not aching, and after some games I was in real pain, usually from bruised ribs, sprained thumbs, and massive headaches.

In my sophomore year, I made the first-string of the varsity team, playing both offense and defense. This was probably my best year as a ball player. I was in good shape, I knew my team members' strengths and weaknesses well; I understood how to work with the guards when they were blocking straight or pulling in order to clear a hole. We were a Class C team (under 500 students) and our opponents were mostly small private schools. We won more than half our games most seasons and the scores were always respectable even when we lost, except when we played triple-A Rogers High School on Thanksgiving Day, a game we never won.

One day I remember well, we were playing the Portsmouth Priory, a rich prep school which Bobby Kennedy attended. They were Catholic like us, well-brought up and polite young men. So we thought. However, when we broke from the huddle, the Priory defensive center growled at me and said, "I'm coming right through you, you skinny punk. I'm gonna break your fucking ass." I was totally disconcerted. I had never heard anyone swear on the field, much less threaten another player. It was just not done in the 1950s, especially at Catholic schools. I was familiar with the "dozens" or the trading of insults which were common among black players but even they were careful on the field. Anyway, taking advantage of my shock, he broke through on the first play and made a tackle. The next play was a pass and I barely held him, and we made a first down. The next, an off-tackle play. Four yards. Second down. The next, the guard pulled on a trap play, and the defensive center came through so fast, he nailed the quarterback before he could make the hand-off. Loss of five. Third down and eleven. Terry got up from the ground and looked at me. "What the hell, Mike. You can't handle that guy. You're going to get me killed." We punted.

Mr. Eagan, our line coach, called me over to the bench. "Don't say anything, Hogan. I know that guy has got you intimidated. But this isn't about you. It's about protecting the quarterback. You got your Terry sacked twice and he's vulnerable, out of position when he's throwing a pass or making a hand-off. He could get hurt bad, and then where would the team be? Your job is to get that ball back to him and then protect him.

"That's your only job. Their center is nothing. He's bigger than you, sure. But he's just a tub of lard with a loud mouth. Move him out of the way, pull him by the jersey, push him, and chop his legs out from under him. Insult him, yell at him.

"Come here. Try to get through me." He got down in a three-point stance. As I moved he slapped my helmet, pulled my jersey, yelled and pushed me to the side.

"Use his weight against him; get him off balance. Yell at him. Freak him out. Act like you're crazy. Just do it!"

The next set of offensive plays I followed his advice. Once I elbowed the center up under his helmet and gave him a bloody nose. Another time the quarterback faked a run and I used the lineman's weight to push him in the direction of the fake. As the game progressed, I did other things: I cussed at him, made my eyes so wide that only the whites showed; I yelled, "Agggg!" snagging his jersey under the shoulder pads and pushing him to the side or, if he tried to move around me, dropped and cut him off at the legs. At least twice he complained to the referee that I was holding. Once, during a time-out, I saw him being bawled out by his coach. Each time he got more and more enraged and frustrated, and each time I manipulated him. Finally, he just hauled off and punched me and incurred a 15 yard penalty for unsportsmanlike conduct. We won the game 21-7 and afterwards, my teammates formed a phalanx as we went to the bus because there was a rumor that he and his friends were going to "teach me a lesson" in the parking lot.

When we got on the bus there was jubilation, and Clem Rego, who was the hero with two touchdowns, was being praised and given high fives. Terry, the quarterback who threw the touchdown passes, was also a hero. Me, I was just feeling good that I had survived. Then, one of the big tackles said, "Hey, you prima donnas should remember who protected your asses." Then, Clem said, "Shit, yeah. How about that crazy whiteboy? Craziest whiteboy I ever saw." Then the coach came on board. "Don't let it go to your head, Slick," he said to me. Then to the group, "Listen up. Everyone did a great job today. I'm proud of you all. We'll stop at the Creamery on the way in for hamburgers and milkshakes." And the team roared its approval.

But despite this initial success, I found that the position demanded more of me physically than I was able to deliver. Outweighed in every game, the muscle strain and the constant battering took its toll. Some Sunday mornings I was so sore I could not get out of bed. And I was often still battered, bruised and nursing a sprain from the previous week when the next game rolled around. We ended the season 5-5-1 which was not bad, but certainly not great. We had what the coach called a "respectable season." Still, I was ready for a long overdue rest but we had one more game to play, the traditional Thanksgiving Day contest against Rogers High.

I was more effective as a middle linebacker than as a center and it was on defense that I really shone that day. I found the nickname Slick more appropriate than Crazy Whiteboy and was determined to earn it. But I needed to play smarter, since I had neither the weight nor the resources to play tougher.

Most high school play-books were the same, so by knowing most of the plays I was able to predict quite often the direction of the play. I was able to break up plays before they began calling for blitzes. By spotting a quarterback wetting his fingertips, I would call for a shift to defend against a pass. I was able to see the direction of the play by the way a rookie lineman tilted his shoulders or leaned into his three-point stance, and I had averaged 8-10 tackles per game. But the game against Rogers High School, our city rival, would be tougher. They were a triple-A team, veterans, with a State Championship reputation. Many of them were All-County or All-State picks. We had only two All-County players: our left guard and our fullback. But I had seen films of the Rogers games; I knew their playbook, and I knew that whatever weaknesses or telegraphing appeared, I would be able to take advantage of them. I was an opportunistic player.

That Monday there was a heavy three-hour practice of fundamentals, followed by a pep talk, study of the playbook and watching films. The next day, a timed one-hour scrimmage (which lasted two hours as the coach interrupted with time-outs to make changes, corrections, and give instruction.) On Wednesday there was a light scrimmage with no pads, and then we went to the gym for a pep rally.

The pep rally was held in the sports center which housed our basketball court and our theater stage. On this day it was packed to the rafters not only with the 450 students of De La Salle Academy, the teachers, coaches, secretaries, and maintenance people, but also with parents, local media, and the 380 girls from St. Catherine's Academy, our sister school. Best of all were the cheerleaders, dressed in the team sweaters, jumpers, white socks and tennis shoes. They did a series of routines out on the center of the basketball court, very sexy and suggestive despite the presence of the Christian Brothers and the nuns. We boys didn't take our eyes off of them but, trained to avoid the attention of the monitor, Brother Francis, managed to control our lascivious whoops and whistles and settled for gentlemanly applause. Then, the football team was introduced and veteran players were given their "D" varsity letters and I received my first. The school song was sung by the choir, the cheerleaders led the combined student bodies in chants, and then the head coach, Mr. Peterson, gave a speech, followed by our team captain. It was a heady time, and out in the parking lot afterwards we flirted with the cheerleaders and other girls from St. Catherine's and then went off to the Creamery where we drank the double-rich Awful-Awful ice cream shakes which were so popular with our generation.

The morning of the game was a frosty one. I could smell the preparations for Thanksgiving dinner in the kitchen downstairs. We would have our traditional dinner at one o'clock; the game was at ten. I got up, did some light calisthenics, and then drove with my Dad to the school. There I got dressed and waited while some of the other players got their ankles taped up. When everyone was ready we marched over to Freebody Park in our freshly-laundered home-game uniforms of white and purple, the gold Crusader's helmets in our hands. Our cleats made a rhythmic clacking beat as we walked to the stadium and I felt like a young gladiator, bold and confident, hoping to see a girl along the way that I might impress. I was anxious, too, to see my Dad and my sister and my Grandpa when we ran into the stadium and the home crowd stood and roared their welcome. My mother never attended games, not even this most important one, both because she had to prepare the midday meal but, more importantly, because she could not bear to see me hurt.

I myself felt no anxiety along those lines, although I did have a persistent nagging fear before every game that I would somehow screw up, make a critical mistake that cost us the game, miss a tackle or a block and, especially when my Dad was in the stands, the fear of doing something that would make him ashamed. So, when we entered the stadium to the applause of the crowds and I jostled the players next to me in rough camaraderie, I was nervous and wired and would remain that way until after the first kickoff when I finally made contact with another player and felt that rush of adrenaline which put everything out of mind except for the game.

The biggest discovery in the Rogers game was that, although these players were bigger, heavier, older and more experienced, they were not any tougher than we were. As my Dad told me before the game, "They put their pants on the same way you do, son. One leg at a time." And it was this ordinariness, after the first two or three plays which gave me confidence. Their backs went down when they were tackled. Their passes could be deflected or intercepted. Their All-State offense could be slowed, maybe even stopped, if we followed the simple moves we had learned over and over again in practice.

For me the joy of the game was watching the plays unfold and moving to the right part of the field to contain the play, cut down the interference, or make a tackle. Play after play I was usually in the right spot, moving fluidly, and once running across the field to chase down a Rogers back. In the third quarter I stopped a spectacular touchdown run ten yards short of the goal line. We held them, and they had to kick a field goal. But we still lost, as the pundits predicted. The Rogers team was relentless, well-trained and talented. Their defense held us to a single touchdown, and we allowed them to score five. But, even so, it was a respectable game for a Class C team. It had been predicted that we would lose by forty or more points.

That winter I discovered girls and had my first real date. In the summer I got my driver's license, and spent nights at beach parties, or making out in my Dad's car on Ocean Drive, drinking beer, smoking cigarettes. I may have played an occasional set of tennis but I seldom ran, never worked out, and gradually replaced my jock friends with a wilder set who enjoyed the night life, drag races out at Third Beach in Middletown, and pretty girls.

When August rolled around I was in terrible shape. I couldn't even complete the one mile run (four laps) around Freebody Park and had to walk the last two laps. I still had a good sprint, though. My shoulders were bigger and I had put on a few pounds. But there was no muscle behind the new weight and I slacked off whenever I could during the callisthenic drills. Younger players would sometimes nail me in a scrimmage, and I had more than the occasional leg cramps, torn ligaments, even a concussion, all resulting from a distracted mind and a poorly-conditioned body. My mother chose this time to renew her campaign for me to quit football. She would reiterate each night at dinner how dangerous the game was, and often had a clipping from a newspaper which told of terrible injuries and even deaths of high school athletes. When she asked my father for his support with her argument, he would always reply, "It's up to the boy, Anna. He can quit or he can play; whatever he wants." But I knew that he would have nothing but contempt for me if I quit. And what would I quit for? So that I would have more time to smoke cigarettes and drink beer, hang around with hoodlums and trashy girls? Exactly.

The school year began with a pre-season game called the Rhode Island Round Robin. The goal was to raise money for injured ballplayers. A series of ten-minute quarters were to be played by all the invited teams. These match-ups were by lottery so that you might see a Class B matched up with a Triple A, but it gave the crowds a chance to see all the teams play, even though they were sometimes unequal contests. Still, there were sometimes

121

lively upsets as a less-favored team went on to win the abbreviated contest, mainly because the rival coach thought it too foolish to risk injury to one of his varsity players in a non-league, pre-season game.

De La Salle was allocated a Class A team from Providence in the lottery. Coach Peterson and Assistant Coach Eagan were excited. They both wanted to start off the year with a bang, and advised us to play full out, knowing that if we made an impressive showing it would not only make headlines in the sports' pages of our local newspaper, but would give the team momentum in the regular season. I had been replaced by a stockier player at center, but I was first-string defense, playing middle linebacker. It was still my favorite spot, and even after a summer of dissolution, I felt good, wired up for the game. I knew no one in the stands; we were playing a road game, and I felt sure that no one knew me. However, I was mistaken. The coach of the opposing teams had seen films of several games and one of those showed a linebacker who had a suspiciously high percentage of tackles and interceptions. He knew who this player was, knew that he anticipated plays from the common play book, and had noted his jersey number.

So, after this cocky, out-of-shape linebacker had successfully read a couple of plays and stopped the runners for minimal yardage, the opposing coach concocted a play which was an end run that began as a trap play, and ended up with a guard, a halfback and a fullback leading a sweep around the left end. Both the guard and the halfback had been instructed to key off me and take me out of the play.

Reading the trap, I moved in the direction of the play, pushed off the block from their left end, and then was out of step when the play moved further out instead of inside. Then the guard nailed me high from the side knocking off my helmet, then the halfback hit me head-on, slamming my head back onto the hard turf as the fullback ran over me and down the field. When the play was over, I was unconscious, and blood was streaming out of my nose and ears. I was carried off the field, taken by ambulance to the hospital and held there for two days of tests and observations. I'd suffered a severe concussion, and a slight cerebral hemorrhage. I was sidelined for the next game.

When the coach asked me to check with the doctor and get a slip certifying that I was fit to play the following week, I began to have second thoughts about returning. I was a junior, planning on going to college, and pursuing a career which would likely be one in which I would use my mind. I didn't know much about the brain but I did know that knocks like the one I had experienced were not good for it. When I saw the doctor, I asked him, and he said, "Well, you've healed nicely and there's no permanent damage. It's unlikely that you'll have a repeat of this injury. You were off-balance, lost your helmet after the first tackle, and the second hit was a lucky one. Still, it's up to you. You decide.'"

I left the office with a note from the doctor which read, "No more football." That satisfied my mother, of course: she asked no more. The head coach, Mr. Peterson, looked at it and said, "Well, that's it, huh? We'll miss you, Mike. You showed a lot of guts out there." Then the line coach, Mr. Eagan came over. "What's the story?" he asked. I started to hand him the paper. He looked me in the eye

123

and said, "I don't want to see a paper. I want to know what the story is."

"The story is...um...the doctor said I couldn't play any more football," I said, feeling the shame rise within me, as I turned away from my own complicity in the decision.

"Well," Mr. Eagan replied, "if that's what the doctor said...."

That November we had our pep rally as usual. This time I attended with some of my wise-guy, beer-drinking classmates and sat at the end furthest away from the football team. We ogled the cheerleaders and made comments. Then, as the coach was reading off the roll of players to receive their "D" varsity letters for the season, I heard my name. I climbed down from the bleachers in a daze, crossed the basketball court and headed for the stage. My former teammates solemnly came to their feet as I passed, and then the rest of the auditorium joined them in giving me a standing ovation. Mr. Eagan took the microphone. "We are giving this varsity letter to Mike Hogan, who was injured in the opening game of the season. His teammates voted for him to receive this honor. Congratulations, Mike" I looked into his eyes and there was no hint of irony. He was being sincere and straight-forward. I was forgiven. It was a moment of grace, and yet as I returned to my seat amid cheers and backslapping, I was never more ashamed.

DE LA SALLE

MY OLD HIGH SCHOOL has been transformed into luxury condominiums now, but one can see the elegance still and imagine the pride of a working class boy chosen to attend there. The carefully-trimmed lawn swept down to tree-lined Bellevue Avenue where the Vanderbilts and the Pierponts, the incredibly rich-before-income-tax, 19th century magnates, had their summer estates.

The inside of the school was impressive as well; the grand staircase with its polished oak, the oil paintings of Colonial governors, the polished railings, and the vaulted ceilings. Christian Brothers in their black robes, crosses tucked into thick leather belts, made their way along the corridors with crisp smoothness as if floating. We felt privileged and I suppose we were, but we also felt captive by a past that was not ours, by a religion which seemed severe and medieval, and by a discipline which far exceeded that in our own modest homes.

The exuberance of Tommy Gough was met with a quick slap by the French teacher, Brother Denis, when Tommy mispronounced the word for pen and then, when asked to repeat it properly, did a credible imitation of the effeminate brother. Brother Peter in English class, a Friar Tuck look-alike, would turn red in the face when anyone made a joke, passed a note, or giggled during the Morning Prayer.

"Come to the front, Mr. Hogan," he'd order.

As I stood in front of him, grinning out of embarrassment, and readying myself for the slap that I knew was coming, he'd raise his right hand.

"Get that cocky grin off your face, or I'll knock it off.!"

And then, as I moved imperceptively to avoid the slap from his right, he'd pop me with his cupped left hand in a resounding smack that could be heard out in the corridor.

I can't remember the slaps ever hurting very much. And we never reported such punishment when we came home. Some boys who made that mistake often found themselves beaten again by their father for whatever offense deserved such punishment from the Brother in the first place. It was also generally accepted that, even if you came from a family which did not indulge in corporal punishment, the punitive attention of the Brothers from De La Salle were part of the price you paid for a good education.

I was something of a class clown so I got more than the average share of slaps. I remember once when Brother Peter left the room during the first period class when we said the Pledge of Allegiance and sang the Star Spangled Banner, deciding I would direct the anthem as a conductor and stood in front of the class using his yardstick as a baton. He came in during the middle of my performance, waited until I was finished, and then whacked me so many times and so hard with the yardstick that he broke it.

The broken yardstick brought forth hoots from the boys and so, more infuriated, he proceeded to strike me about the head and shoulders with his hands.

"Of all the disrespectful, arrogant young men I've ever taught, you take the prize. You...you...."

And, as words failed him and his face reddened with rage, I felt his impotence when confronted with what was essentially no more than youthful irreverence. He could not inculcate in me the simple devotion to God or the Academy or even America which for most children of immigrants such as myself was usually unquestioning. I remember feeling sorry for him as he wiped the sweat from his brow and instructed me to return to my seat. He had lost it and I had won.

"How was school today?" my mother asked when I came home that afternoon. I remember the smile on my face as I said, "I had a great day, Mom."

Breaking Brother Peter was an accomplishment. He never struck me after that. Perhaps I modified my tendencies as class clown as well, but I don't think so. Nor did he stop striking other students. However, some of the zest had gone out of his slaps when he struck the other boys. And, while he never raised his hand to me again, he had replaced physical aggression with verbal. Once, I recall, he told me, "Mr. Hogan, you have a cavalier attitude." For a few days I went around thinking of myself as one of the Musketeers, a swashbuckling equestrian, until I looked up the word in the dictionary.

While Brother Peter had been put in his place by passive resistance and quiet dignity in the face of impotent fury, there remained one nemesis that could not be dealt with so easily. He was a priest and a Latin teacher who utilized physical aggression in a more manly way. Father Gallagher would call you up to give the declension of a Latin noun or to conjugate a verb in front of the class. If you missed the ablative plural of *mensa*, or the third person subjunctive of *amare*, he would tell you to tighten up, and then punch you solidly in the stomach. He'd smile as he did this, and you were expected to smile stoically back, wrack your brains, and then try to recite perfectly the second time. If you did not do your homework for Father Gallagher's class, you'd better have a cast iron stomach. I endured him for three years of Latin and I remember that for all of us boys in that class, sit-ups were considered every bit as important as memorizing declensions and conjugations.

Father Gallagher considered himself to be one of the cool members of the faculty. He drove a Harley Davidson to work. He would offer you coffee if you went to his office for counseling. On weekends he could often be found out by the beaches where some of us went to drink beer and make out with the local girls from Saint Catherine's. It wasn't until a wild beach party one spring break during our junior year that we found out what he was up to. Giving a sermon at St. Augustine Church on purity and abstinence, he asked our parents: "And where was your Johnny on Saturday night? Your Michael? And where was your Mary? Your Cindy?" looking at each of our parents in turn. "I'll tell you where," he roared. "Out in the dunes at Second Beach drinking beer and indulging in God knows what impurities."

He'd been parking his Harley somewhere out of sight and then creeping up on the campfire to record who was there. I never trusted him after that, and no longer was amused by his manly punches even when I was not their focus.

In our senior year, a sickly boy by the name of Gavin was called up in front of the Latin class. He missed the line he was supposed to translate from Virgil. I remember it well. *Sic volvere Parcas*, which had to do with the Fates spinning the web of predestination for Aeneus and his crew in that unforgettable epic of the founding of Rome. "Umph," Gavin was struck the hard punch to the breadbasket. And then his face paled and he collapsed in a heap on the floor. The local fire department was called (they operated the EMT service) and with sirens and much excitement Gavin was taken to Newport Hospital. It was rumored that his appendix had burst. At any rate he never returned to De La Salle. Shortly thereafter our Latin teacher was gone as well to become a chaplain at a retirement home for nuns.

By the end of my senior year, corporal punishment was a thing of the past. We used to joke about the good old days and how the new kids coming up had it so easy. Verbal abuse continued, of course, and sarcasm became a much more finely-honed instrument on the part of the Brothers. We were tolerant of that and would smile when one of them would suggest that if we didn't do better on exams then we'd most certainly end up as buck privates peeling potatoes in the army. Or, when not paying attention in class, another would suggest that our thoughts of sex would almost certainly lead us to "a hell, where sex would be all we'd ever be able to think of." We knew they were dealing as best they could with the new restrictions which had disarmed them of their old weapons. Sarcasm involved much more thought and practice than corporal punishment, so we appreciated their efforts. We would wince when they did not pull it off, and inwardly applaud a good quip even if one of our clique was the victim.

"So," said Brother Leo, when I was staring out the window during history class in May of my senior year. "Are you already deep into your own masterfully-written book, Mr. Hogan, or could we entice you back to our own poor text?"

I smiled back condescendingly. *Not bad, Brother Leo. Keep practicing.*

A WRITER'S ALMANAC

NEWPORT, RHODE ISLAND, IN my memory is a mist-shrouded isle in the Atlantic, accessible only by ferry or bridge from the mainland: isolated, insular, with a population of less than thirty thousand. It is a place of white beaches, warm currents, peaceful bays, and golden sunshine where the bells of St. Mary's and St. Augustine's ring out in the seaside streets each Sunday, where girls in white dresses walk in May processions, and golden boys in school blazers and simonized Chevy convertibles cruise the downtown streets. It was, in my teen years in the late 1950s and early 1960s, as free a place as existed for teenagers in the United States. We had our own cars to drive or those of our parents, we had beaches on both sides of the island, as well as abandoned homes and old estates vacated in the winter by the Vanderbilts and Astors which we could explore and have private parties in. We had a police force which tolerated the wildest of us. None of my friends ever got arrested for drag racing, or drinking underage, or fighting, or vandalism, although most of us had committed those misdemeanors by the time we were seventeen.

There were some things which held us in check. We were mostly Catholics and, while we varied in our degrees of belief, church attendance was compulsory and that included Saturday afternoon confession and Holy Communion each Sunday morning. If you did not rise from the pew and go to the altar to receive your wafer of unleavened bread, it was assumed you had been up to something Saturday night which had resulted in mortal sin. And you'd better be prepared to explain that dereliction not only to parents but to well-meaning friends and siblings, as well as to the nun who taught you 8th grade English, and the priest who taught you 10th grade Latin, all of whom were in the congregation and witnessed your absence from the Communion rail.

You could smoke, of course, and drink alcohol if you chose, but for those of us who played sports, those indulgences soon became apparent on the basketball court or the football field, as winded and exhausted, we were pulled over to the sidelines by the coach, castigated and humiliated, and then forced to take ten laps. The temptation to cheat on the rules was unlikely to be indulged in again.

I would not say that sex was non-existent. But the fear of pregnancy (this was before the pill) and the heavy Catholic training surrounded every potential sexual encounter with a caution and a reserve which was palpable. So we dated, went to dances and movies, "made out," which consisted of little more than heavy kissing unless you were prepared to give a blow by blow account to Father Gallagher that Saturday in confession or, assuming it was already Saturday night, risk the gauntlet of relatives and friends when you failed to kneel on Sunday morning to receive the Host.

Most of our controls were internal and social. No one I knew had ever been beaten by his parents in any cruel way, although corporal punishment was not uncommon. Few of us were even denied the use of the family car. We had a great deal of free, unstructured time from the age of thirteen until we went on to college. We had wild friends and conservative ones. We did risky things like jumping off thirty-foot cliffs into quarry pond, or drag-racing cars along the beaches at high speeds, or taking sail boats out in nor'easter storms and high seas. No one I knew ever drowned, or was in a James Dean-type car crash. No one I knew was ever booked by the police; the cops simply yelled at us, gave us a warning and threatened to tell our parents. There were no juvenile courts or detention centers.

While the town was generally conservative, there was an element which smiled at youthful exuberance. When the seventy-year-old President Eisenhower came to spend the summer when I was fourteen, we grimaced at his poor taste when he and his staff drove by in a fleet of Edsels which was a car most of us considered ridiculously old-fashioned even when new. However, when the young Senator John Kennedy raced around the Ocean Drive in a '55 Corvette, evading the secret service contingent and the police, even our parents smiled tolerantly, although more sedate residents were scandalized.

Having a priest who was a friend was commonplace and the sexual abuse tales we hear about today were highly unlikely then since we hung around in groups and the priest was as visible in his sexuality (or lack of it) as we were. The priest knew who was dating whom, who drank too much at a party, and who had a problem with depression. He could be trusted not to tell our parents almost anything, short of a suicide threat. By our senior year everyone I knew also had a girlfriend, usually called a "steady," for whom the advent of university spelled a deepening of the relationship, or a prelude for tears and final partings. The university loomed as the great unknown and a termination of island life since we had to leave Newport and, with employment opportunities there so limited, would likely never return.

A few of us were considered "bright" in school but most were ordinary. "Bright" was sometimes dangerous because you could be singled out and exposed to ridicule, seen as a suck-up, and usually end up with the bulk of the work on school projects. Some were considered "dumb" (this was before the concepts and terminology of learning disabilities entered the educational system) and they were treated with gentle tolerance rather than contempt, although like Rudolph they were never asked to play in reindeer games.

It was cool to be a jock, whether in basketball, baseball or football. It was cool to have a talent easily recognizable like music or art or writing. In was also cool in this beatnik era to simply "be cool," which was an indefinable quality characterized by not taking anything too seriously, knowing something about jazz music and Ginsberg's poetry, being against the atomic bomb, and not caring about social events or who was dating whom. Genuine beatniks were merely an exaggeration of our own coolness, we felt, since we all shared this style of appearing nonchalant, taking nothing too seriously, and pretending to be unmoved by the rejections and conflicts which raged around us as tidal in force as our hormones.

For those of us who attended Catholic schools, a quick wit, a gift for self-dramatization and a caustic sarcasm characterized the best of our teachers. We knew they could slice us to ribbons with their tongues if we did not come to classes prepared. We also knew that they loved their subjects and, when they were "on," could be more fascinating than television. Public school kids, who were not so fortunate, often wondered why we liked school so much. Looking back now, I see that it was the one place where we were taken seriously. Our English teachers read our essays as if what we wrote really mattered. Our coaches looked at each game as if it were a monumental (never-to-be-repeated) contest of will, intelligence and skill. If we skipped a class, we were missed. If we acted stupidly, impolitely or indifferently, we were castigated. If we did something well, we were acknowledged.

At a time when it was so important to be "cool" and indifferent, school was the only place we saw true involvement, concern and passion from adults. Our parents were generally too busy with their businesses, their professions, and getting ahead in those economic boom times, to pay us more than passing attention. Our actual learning was something they did not take too seriously (although grades mattered) and our feeble attempts at athletic glory in the mini-arenas of our small Catholic school did not merit more than passing condescension. Yet the ceremony of receiving the varsity letter, the intense passion of the basketball and football games, the honor society awards, publication in the school magazine, all gave a semblance of value and significance to what we did.

Looking back now on those days to see what remains of the tatters of memories, I reach into the smoke of those years which once burned so brightly, to bring out...what? A much beloved friend? An A in my history class? No, what I bring out is the day I was chosen to be on the varsity football team, the exalted feeling of being chosen, coupled almost immediately with the certain knowledge that I would not be good enough, that I would let my team down: a 150 pound skinny kid with a lot of heart but little talent. The next memory is the time I intercepted a ball in the end zone as it spiraled downward in the October sun and then the slow-motion pivot as the opposing players raced towards me, then the mindless race along the sideline, not feeling their blows as I slipped through their tackles to the thirty yard line, the forty, the forty-five, then past mid-field where I was finally brought down by a fast cornerback. As he helped me up, he said: "Not bad for a chickenshit white boy." It was a moment of ecstasy, as T.S. Eliot would say, that was "in and out of time" and each October as I walk across the browning grass of a football field, I feel that tingle of recognition that the world is more frightening and fragile and amazing than Horatio could have conceived in any of his philosophies.

Back into the memories as the fog rises across Narragansett Bay and the deep-throated foghorn echoes against the cliffs. I walk to school on a spring morning, the wind containing just a remnant of the winter's chill, the jonquils and tulips putting their green stalks up through the muddy earth. It is an ordinary day. I am in the tenth grade and am thinking about the Latin translation I was assigned and I know that I have not got the ending exactly right, then there's the algebra homework that is only half-completed.

My friend, Tommy O'Grady catches up with me at the school parking lot. He has a girlfriend, I do not. He is rich, owns his own car, and wears elegantly-fitted clothes. He plays quarterback; I am a mere linebacker. Still, Tommy is my friend.

Today he tells me, "I was out with Sandra last night. She told me that Katie Sullivan really likes you."

Katie Sullivan. I have thought about her in Latin class, in algebra class, in history class.... Katie Sullivan, Katie Sullivan. I picture her at St. Catherine's Academy in her plaid jumper, hanging out with her friends. She is a vivacious redhead: stylish, trim, with a smile that lights up any room. She has flirted with me in the past, but then she flirts with everybody, and it is never serious. Katie always acts as if you're the most important person in the world when you're around her. Finally, it is lunchtime. I seek out Tommy O'Grady.

I try to be casual. "So, what exactly did she say, Tommy?" I ask.

"Who?" he says.

"What did your girlfriend say about Katie Sullivan?" I ask patiently.

"Just that she liked you."

The bell rings and I see that's all I'm going to get out of the thick-headed Irishman I call my friend. But, to be fair, that's probably all she said. I spend the rest of the afternoon lost in a daze, a vision of us riding together in my father's car, driving out to the cliffs above Narragansett Bay. Her sliding closer to me across the front seat....

That night I called her and then hung up as soon as her mother answered. I got ready to call again, rehearsing what I would say. "Could I speak to Katie, please?" Or, "This is Michael; could I talk to Katie, please?" Or, "Hi, Mrs. Sullivan, is Katie home?" Finally, I called and Katie answered the phone herself! I hung up in embarrassment and panic. I made a couple more half-hearted attempts and then, finally, I gave it up.

When I saw her the next day at her father's hardware store, I mentioned the fact that I had tried calling her the night before. "And you hung up?" she asked. "Yeah," I said sheepishly. "My sister was hanging around the phone and I couldn't really talk."

"Well, tonight I'll call you!" she said enthusiastically. "Just take the phone and go into the bedroom. Say it's private; that's what I do."

Thus began a telephone relationship that to this day I'm sure holds the record for time on-line. Katie and I would literally talk for hours in the weeks and months that followed. Neither of us would be willing to hang up first. My mother would warn me to get back to my homework; my father would bellow about me tying up the line; my sister would plead with me to hang up and help her with her math, but nothing would avail. Katie Sullivan and I were addictive telephone companions. We talked about everything: school, gossip, sports, love, girlfriends, boyfriends, music, cinema, our future lives, dysfunctional parents, annoying siblings, politics, the atomic bomb, poetry and novels. It was the second time I lost myself in the timelessness of time. I experienced pure ecstasy as her honeyed voice poured its sweet syllables into my ear, more musical than a Mozart symphony. It echoes still, down through those lost and never-to-be-repeated years.

Then comes the day, as you know it must, when everything turns to dust in my mouth. Katie, a year older than I, had gone on to college and found a Yale boyfriend. I had suffered a serious injury in a pre-season game and no longer played football. I get accepted to Harvard but the

State of Rhode Island scholarship which I am awarded is not enough to cover tuition. I am looking at my "backup" schools: Boston College, Providence College, University of Rhode Island, Stonehill College, with little enthusiasm. I am reminded of another T.S. Eliot poem: "And that's the way the world ends, not with a bang but a whimper." And here I am wimping at the end of my wimpy senior year, and it is May and the air is sticky with humidity. It is hot and I have no energy, no love, and no joy. But then June comes with graduation and summer work. So, I go out each morning with a landscaping crew to earn the extra money that I will need for books and fees for the little Catholic liberal arts college in North Easton, Massachusetts.

Stonehill College, set back in the remote Massachusetts woods outside of Brockton, was much to my surprise a rather idyllic place. I think of it now as a little patch of Thoreau-like sanctuary where I walked over a rustic wooden bridge after classes into the autumn woods and wrote poetry and essays and stories in my notebooks. My favorite class was Freshman Composition with a professor by the name of Peter Luchesi who carefully and critically read everything I wrote each week, made marginal suggestions (not corrections) on my papers, and always an encouraging comment. This in itself was quite unusual because Freshman Comp was a crowded class and employed a teaching assistant who read most of the papers. One day in November Mr. Luchesi called me up to his desk. "I really liked your last essay. I think I can get it published, if you're interested."

Then he began to quote parts of the essay to me; explained how he shared it in the faculty lounge, and how he sent it to a friend of his in Boston who edited a magazine. And then he told me how his friend wrote back, suggested some minor changes, and offered to publish it and pay me! And suddenly I could actually smell the elixir of roses where they blossomed outside of the Fine Arts Building. I could hear the sparrows splashing in the fountain. I could see the pride and the kindness in the hazel eyes of my professor as he smiled and said, "Why do you look so surprised? Surely, Michael, you've known that you were a writer for quite some time."

I burn with combustible joy. A writer! I am both exalted and transcendent. I have been lifted out of the rat pack of failed athletes and broken-hearted lovers, out of the humiliation of middle class not-quite-enough-money for Harvard, out of the hospitalization for the brutal tackle in the long-ago September, into the warm interior of a life of fulfillment. The courtly and generous-spirited Mr. Luchesi, who touched so many students with genuine interest and caring, brought me to a life that would, even in its worst days, be full of blessings. "There will never be," he told me in his kindly voice, "anything ugly or sad, depressing or crushing, that you cannot make beautiful and life-affirming simply by writing about it." And so it was, and is.

A SOFT RAIN WAS FALLING

Render unto Caesar the things that are Caesar's
And unto God the things that are God's.
--Matthew 22:21

THE YEAR WAS 1916; it was Monday after Easter in the dreary streets of downtown Dublin. Inside the church the air was rich with odors of lilies, beeswax candles and incense. The priest had finished reading the Gospel of St. John from the left side of the altar, and now descended the marble steps and approached the Communion rail.

"Before you leave this church, I want you all to know one thing," he addressed those who were waiting for the Last Blessing. "Remember this. When Jesus showed the Pharisees the coin and said, 'Render unto Caesar what is Caesar's and unto God what is God's, he spoke of our duty to those who rule our country. The legitimate ruler of Ireland is the British Empire. Those of you who have bothers or husbands or fathers planning to revolt against the government are in danger of great sin. It is your solemn duty as Catholics to stop them, and to warn them that their souls are in danger and that, if they persist in this foolishness, they are to be excommunicated."

Outside a soft rain had fallen. The Uprising, planned for Easter Sunday had been postponed for tactical reasons much to the chagrin of the poet Padraic Pearse, who knew the importance of symbolism. To begin the rebirth of a free Irish nation on the same day of Christ's resurrection would have been memorable. Still, there was no help for it. But this morning finally, the die had been cast. The rebels began their march up O'Connell Street headed for the General Post Office where they would make their headquarters.

British soldiers in the vicinity of Church Street were nervous. Some had fought in France and were veterans of the Great War, but others were fresh recruits and had never seen combat before. It may have been that the young soldiers wanted to make an impression on the veterans or that they were simply scared, but when the congregants streamed from the church, the soldiers opened fire. Several women lay dead in the streets after the fusillade; then the British artillery shelled the nearby buildings whose ruins would conveniently cover the massacre. The firing between the Irish rebels and the English troops would continue for most of the week before the surrender, and the British soldiers, frustrated in their attempts to extricate rebels from the Dublin buildings, would go on killing women, children and old men, most notably on Church Street, North King Street, and South Summer Street. When the Uprising was finally over, there were more innocent civilians lying dead than British troops or Irish rebels.

The British held an inquiry but no one was ever punished for the massacre. The Uprising was crushed, the leaders hanged, and others placed on the fugitive terrorist list by the British government. Bridget Steward, age 11, Martha Kelly, age 12, Gerald Hogan, Annie Walsh and one hundred and fifty others were interred in the local cemeteries and forgotten to history. But they were not forgotten by my grandfather or any of the others who witnessed the murders that week.

My grandfather immigrated to the New World and, after the death of his wife in childbirth, raised his three daughters Mary, Abbie and (my mother) Anna, by himself until he could afford to bring his sisters over from the Old Country. He never remarried. He never forgot North King Street Massacre and the other murders that followed. And he never forgave the priest who sided with the British and told the women to go out and stop the Uprising.

He had told me this story not once but a dozen times as a child. Many times he was interrupted by my mother who felt it was inappropriate. She also felt that it could undermine my faith. But he always replied, "The boy has got to know his history, Anna. How else can we make sure this kind of thing does not happen again and again? He's got to see that the Church as an institution is fallible and that some of the mistakes they make are deadly."

My grandfather was anti-clerical and anti-institutional. It was why he did not come to my Baptism, or my Confirmation. It was why, although he attended Mass, he always stood in the back of the church, and never received Communion or went to Confession. If asked why he did not leave the Catholic Church and become a Protestant he would quote Brendan Behan saying, "I refuse to embrace a religion founded upon the testicles of an English King!" He disliked priests intensely and spoke of then with a curled-lip contempt. "A sorry bunch of black-skirted sissies," he'd roar at the slightest provocation, "who sold Ireland to keep their benefice."

You've heard it said that time heals all wounds, but in my grandfather's case that did not prove to be so. In that, he was not so different from his contemporaries. Among the Irish I knew as a child, the saying seemed more Anglo-Saxon than Celtic. Our neighbors nursed grudges for generations and they clung to their romantic attachments with equal fervor. So it was no surprise to me that my grandfather never re-married, and that he raised his three daughters himself. Or that the middle sister (who was my mother) should call me one weekend when I was off at college and beg me to come home. Her news was that my grandfather, at the ripe age of 81, had suffered a stroke which was likely to be fatal, and that he had refused to allow a priest in the house to administer the Last Rites.

The living room was full of women when I arrived. My mother's sisters, Abbey and Mary, my great-aunts Molly and Bessie were gathered together clucking like pullet hens about the old rooster upstairs whom they called "Himself."

The plan was simple. I was to go upstairs and hold the old man's hand. Meanwhile, they would call the parish church, secure the services of a young priest, and sneak him into the house. When my grandfather dozed off, the good Father would administer the Last Rites.

"Sure," said Aunt Bessie. "Himself is a mere shell after the stroke. He's only a shadow of Himself and it should be no trouble to settle him down."

I had my doubts. But being the good Catholic boy that I was, and trained in obedience to the nuns (and thus any woman who spoke with authority), I trudged up the stairs. The wreck which was my grandfather lay sprawled in the bed, one side paralyzed, and the left side of his face drooping sadly. He was obviously not long for this world. I took his hand and we sat and talked about school and the

Jesuits who were teaching me philosophy up at Boston College. I had transferred there after two years at Stonehill. The Jesuits were the only group of teachers he tolerated because, as he put it, "They actually work for a living."

Downstairs I could hear the murmuring of the women and suddenly the crisp voice of a young man. The priest had arrived from the parish church. I hope that my grandfather's hearing had deteriorated and that he would soon tire and go to sleep, but instead his hand tightened on mine. Looking me straight in the eye, he commanded: "Tell me, Bucko, is there a priest in my house?" I wasn't really afraid of him, I don't think. Although his grip was like a vise and his rage was palpable. But I just couldn't see lying to the only patriarch I'd known as he lay helpless on his deathbed. Besides, what could possibly happen? So, I said, "Yes, Grandpa, there is. There's a priest on his way up to give you the last Rites."

"Over my dead body!" he snorted. "Get me my suit and...my shillelagh."

I didn't think to hesitate. The old revolutionary of 1916 was back: fierce, and flashing eternal righteousness. I help him put on his three-piece tweed suit that had been pressed for his funeral: baggy trousers, suspenders, vest and jacket in the style of half a century before. I handed him the massive black briar walking stick that he called his shillelagh. Then, one arm about my shoulder, the other leaning heavily on the cane, he wended his way slowly to the top of the stairs.

"I'll have no priest in my house!" he shouted to the gathered women and young curate below.

"Oh, Jesus, Mary and Joseph!" cried Aunt Bessie.

"It's Himself out of bed and the boy bold as brass by his side," confirmed Aunt Molly.

"Oh, be careful, Father," warned Aunt Bridget. "He's a terrible dangerous man with no love for priests."

The curate, Father Young, a pale and refined representative of English stock, was unintimidated by these Celtic screeches.

"Now, now," said Father Young as he headed up the stairs. "Now, now."

"Now, now, yerself, ye bloody English hypocrite!" yelled my grandfather, swinging his blackthorn cudgel and holding on to me for support. "Get out of my damn house or I'll knock you into Kingdom Come!"

The priest continued up the stairs oblivious to the warning and insensible of any danger.

"Father," I warned. "He'll do it, you know. I think you'd better go."

"Now, now, son," the priest said, his arms crossed over the Host he held to his breast. "I've dealt with these old folks before and their bark is usually worse than their bite. Just step aside."

I managed to move a fraction of an inch as the heavy briar stick came crashing down on the hapless priest. I fell to one side, my grandfather crashing down on top of me, as the priest spun crazily down the stairs where he ended up unconscious on the landing like a rag doll.

"Now, now," said my grandfather looking down at the bundle of black cloth which had been the priest. "Render that unto Caesar, if ye don't mind." With those words he lay back and closed his eyes in peace.

There was a soft rain falling when the ambulance came. As they brought the stretcher out, the neighbors gathered around to take a last look at my grandfather, survivor of revolutions, and benighted neighborhood character. But it was not an old revolutionary they saw bundled up under the blankets. It was the pale face of the English priest, suffering from a broken collarbone and lost dignity. My grandfather lay asleep with a smile of intense satisfaction in his room at the top of the stairs. He would live there for three more years, the stuff of legends, until he died in his sleep: unrepentant, unshriven, priestless and at peace in his eighty-fourth year to heaven.

A TALE OF TWO PRESIDENTS

NEWPORT, R.I. WAS THE summer residence for Dwight D. Eisenhower beginning in 1958 and ending in 1960. The home, now called "the Eisenhower House," is located in Fort Adams State Park and rented out for wedding receptions and other gala events. When I was a kid the house was a part of Brenton Village, the naval officer's residences for Cruiser-Destroyer Fleet Atlantic, adjacent to the old fort itself.

I was dating Cindy Hooper, the daughter of a naval commodore at the time and she lived two blocks away from Ike's home. Each day I would pass by a Marine guard by the name of Joe Ruszkowski on my Schwinn bike as he gave me a smart salute. Then I would drive up the hill, past the house where Mamie and Ike lived. It was a gorgeous old house. Built in the 1800s by a noted Newport architect named Hunt, it was a stately wooden mansion of three stories, yellow with white trim, and a gray slate roof. It has a wrap-around porch with a view of Narragansett Bay and Newport Harbor bordered by a wide rolling lawn. Sometimes I would see Ike out on the front lawn practicing his putting. Golf was his passion in those days.

More often than not, there would be a motorcade going out the front gate of Brenton Village headed to the Newport Country Club where he spent most of his free time playing in a twosome with a cabinet member or a foursome with business tycoons. What amused us kids in

148

those days was that his official car the first year was the 1958 Ford Edsel which we all considered a very uncool vehicle. This was a time when most kids were very style conscious in the matter of cars, and the 1958 Impala and Corvette, the Ford Thunderbirds, the Plymouth Fury and even the Pontiac Chieftain were considered very stylish by most of us. But the Ford Edsel? It was—like its body design—decidedly square. The Edsel, like Ike himself, was clearly from a generation that was passé and, while we didn't exactly see it coming in 1958, the youthful Kennedy was already being groomed for his position and change was in the wind.

But back to Ike. He was for me and for most of us who had families connected to the military (and in one way or another everyone in Newport did), one of the most famous generals of World War II. I took great delight in spotting him on quiet afternoons when he would be seen sitting on his front porch with John Foster Dulles or his brother Allen smoking Camel cigarettes and having heated discussions. One was Secretary of State and the other was the CIA chief. I knew both their faces from the newspapers and slowed down to give them a wave as I passed by. Ike always returned my waves and sometimes if he was not deep in a discussion would yell, "Hey, kid! How is it going?" Invariably I would reply. "Just fine, Mr. President. See yuh!" and then pedaled off to my date. I never did see Richard Nixon who was the vice-president then. I don't think he ever came to Newport. And after 1960, Ike would never return.

"I am not the Catholic candidate for President. I am the Democratic Party's candidate for President who happens to be a Catholic. I do not speak for my Church on public matters—and the Church does not speak for me." On Tuesday, November 8, 1960, Kennedy narrowly defeated Richard Nixon by 2/10 of a percentage point to become the 35th president of the United States.

On January 20, 1961, we all sat around the television as Kennedy took the oath of office, and then reminded us that "the torch has been passed to a new generation." We were reminded again as we watched the eighty-six-year-old Robert Frost fumble with his wind-blown notes before finally reciting a memorized poem instead of the inaugural piece he had written.

That summer (which would be my last as a formal resident of Newport) my father got a call that President John F. Kennedy and his wife Jacqueline would be hosting a party at the new "Summer White House" at Hammer-smith Farm. They were expecting hundreds of guests on the forty-eight-acre property which was the home of the Jackie's parents, a Victorian mansion with twenty-eight rooms and two large guest cottages. So commodious was the location that the young couple welcomed 2,000 guests to their wedding reception seven years before.

Kennedy was a U.S. Congressman then and he had gotten married at St. Mary's Church on Spring Street. I remember both my father and mother being upset because our local church a block away, St. Augustine's Church, was the Bouvier parish. We would have had a front seat to all the activities. Unfortunately that was not to be. But the procession from St. Mary's to the reception at Hammersmith drove past our house which was located on Harrison Avenue, the beginning of the famed Ocean Drive. There were Cadillacs and Ford Town Cars, I remember, and even a Rolls Royce. But not a single Edsel. The guests were entertained by the Meyer Davis Orchestra which played "I married an Angel."

The local caterers and suppliers were contracted to bring the finest food and drink to this latest party and my father was consulted about the flowers, plants and other ornaments to be used to decorate the mansion and the grounds. Both families were multi-millionaires ever since Jackie's mother had married the wealthy stockbroker Hugh Auchincloss who owned the mansion, so money for this summer affair was plentiful.

My father was also asked by the Auchuncloss estate manager to locate "good looking and polite young men" who knew how to drive expensive vehicles and park them on lawns. That description, of course, fit only the handful of boys who worked on the estates during the summer, had drivers' licenses, had driven luxury cars for the owners and were trusted. So a dozen of us were hired as valet parkers to ease the cars of the guests (carefully) into slots on the rolling lawns.

There were Jaguars, Rolls Royces, Masaratis, Cadillacs, Mercedes and Lincolns. There were also Bentleys, Bugattis, Aston-Martins and Duesenburgs. Many of the cars were worth hundreds of thousands of dollars, a handful were priceless. So we were not only careful, but made note of which car we parked and who the owner was so that we could fetch it quickly when that person was ready to leave the party and have it delivered safely to the front door of the mansion.

This was no easy task. And the boys were very competitive because the gratuities were so significant they could pay for books and fees for a semester at a good college. The lowest denomination given was usually a five, but more often it was a ten or a twenty and once a cool hundred when the guest was in his cups. But one had to be sharp, quick and smooth. One had to remember the vehicle type and color that the guest had ("My Jag, son," or "My old Dusie, please," another would offer), and its approximate location on a 40+ acre property. One had to locate the car (there were no beepers in those days to help out), figure out how the ignition and gear shift worked (some were mounted on the left side in the European fashion, some had floor ignition switches, others had special locking devices), get it out from the closely parked spot without a scratch, and deliver it to the owner.

Although some guests left earlier, it was about 2 AM when they began to depart in any numbers. There was the chatting with the hostess on the front porch which gave us time to recognize and scout the next car. Then we would take off and search down the rows of hundreds of vehicles to find the one we needed. I spotted the owner of a 1938 maroon Packard which was a car I truly loved and remembered. I took off in a sprint knowing I had left it parked at the edge of a rose garden at the far end of a hedged enclosure. As I was turned the corner around the shrubbery, something lifted me up in the air and threw me violently to the ground. I looked up. A beefy linebacker-type stood over me glaring. "Let's see some ID, right now!" he ordered. Grunting with pain I reached into my back pocket, extracted my driver's license, and gave it to him.

"You live here in Newport, I see," he said. "Hmm. Parking cars, are you?

"That's right."

"Well, next time take it easy. Walk fast, don't run. We don't know who the hell you are when you come out of the bushes like that. The President is here, you know."

Used to the loose security of Eisenhower inside the naval base, I had ignored the fact that this was a private residence and there were dozens of Secret Services people on the property. I had seen them of course when they vetted us prior to our being hired and then again when we showed up for work. But they had faded into the dark as they evening progressed and I had forgotten they were out prowling the grounds.

I would see the Secret Service on two more occasions. In the summer of 1962 when I was taking a landscaping truck to a job at Bailey's Beach, a 1957 Corvette came flying past me doing 50 in a 35 mile-an-hour zone. Wearing a blue windbreaker, his brown hair flying in the wind, with five-year-old Caroline beside him, JFK was putting distance between himself and the men assigned to protect him. They caught up with him a good three minutes after he reached the parking lot of the private beach and had already lifted Caroline from the front seat of the sports car and headed for the lounge. Kennedy loved his freedom and indulged it whenever he had a chance. It often seemed he valued it than he valued security.

The last time I would encounter the Secret Service was at Boston College where Kennedy had been invited to give the commemoration speech at the Centennial celebration of the university. I had been invited because I was a senator in student government at the time. I was allowed to sit in the reserved rows, and then to meet the President briefly before he left campus. I was astounded at how accessible he was. For this event I was not even vetted. I just showed my ID, was given a lapel badge by the university and allowed to pass through.

President Pusey from Harvard was there, the Archbishop of Boston, the president of Boston College, Father John Walsh, and several others. What I remember most was that by this time his distinctive accent had become one of the signal differences between him and other speakers we would hear on the radio and TV. He got up to speak after the applause died down.

"I am glad to be back here in Boston," he said. "Where people pronounce the words the way they're spelled." The crowd roared. No one, in Boston or anywhere else in New England, spoke with that accent. It was uniquely Kennedy.

He went on to speak of the recently-published papal encyclical *Pacem in Terris* (Peace on Earth), the last message of John XXIII to the world, for he would die of cancer two months later. In it the Pope spoke of the importance of social justice and the message of Christ to feed the hungry; he spoke of the destruction of wars and how we had the power to end them, and he spoke of the responsibility of "all men and women of good will" to unite with those of other faiths and with non-believers to make the world a more just, more equitable and safer place for our children. As Kennedy succinctly put it:

That document surely shows that on the basis of one great faith and its traditions there can be developed counsel on public affairs that is of value to all men and women of good will. As a Catholic I am proud of it and as an American I have learned from it.

As he and his aides were leaving he passed us collegiate "senators" in the reviewing line and shook our hands. "Great speech, Mr. President," I said.

He smiled, looked at my name tag, and then directly into my eyes. With perfect timing and aplomb, he delivered a classic example of the Kennedy wit, one I have yet to see recorded elsewhere.

"It was a pleasure, Michael. As I was telling Dr. Pusey, I love centennials. We already celebrated *three* at my alma mater!"

The date was April 20, 1963. Less than seven months later America's only Catholic president would be dead from an assassin's bullet in Dallas.

KISSED BY ALLEN GINSBERG

MY COLLEGE YEARS WERE erratic and irregular and my love for the drink didn't help any in these early years before sobriety. After two years Stonehill and I departed company. I went to Boston College for a semester, then a semester at Boston University, and finally finished both my B.A. and an MFA at the University of Arizona years later where I studied with some of the finest poets and writers of the Sixties. My mentor and advisor was Richard Shelton, but I also got to work with Steve Orlen, Ed Abbey, William Stafford, W.S. Merwin, Seamus Heaney, Francine Prose, and Marge Piercy. In 1975 I was awarded the prestigious National Endowment for the Arts Fellowship for Creative Writing as well as two Pushcart Prizes and I was invited to give guest readings and one-day classes at colleges universities throughout the U.S.

I consider myself a minor poet and do not have a great deal of ego attached to what I do. While my work appears occasionally in literary journals, including the *Paris Review* and *American Poetry Review*, it has yet to be seen in *Harper's* or the *New Yorker*. Several textbooks and anthologies carry one fortuitous poem of mine entitled "Spring" which has been reprinted enough to garner me sufficient royalties to buy a mountain bike.

When I die, I will join the ranks of Clough, Lovelace, Herrick and the obscure but prolific Leigh Hunt whose haunting poem "Jenny Kissed me" sums up what I love best about minor poets: their ability to hang in there as a tentative trembling note amidst the grand symphonies of Milton and Keats, Browning and Eliot. If you hang in long enough and don't embarrass too many people with your pretensions, you'll get invited places and might even be chosen to appear on stage with one of the masters to fill out a program.

It was on one such occasion, a conference of small press editors and publishers back in the mid-Seventies, that I first met Allen Ginsberg. The event was a conference at California State College which you would assume was somewhere in that eponymous state on the west coast. However, you'd be mistaken. It was actually in California, Pennsylvania. It was a small liberal arts college hidden in the rolling hills which border the Monongahela River.

I was a member of a trio of poets which included Dianne Wakowski and Allen Ginsberg. Our contract required us to each give a couple of workshops to writers, editors and graduate students during the three day conference. Each night there was to be a poetry presentation from one of us. On Thursday night Diane would give a reading to a small group in the library; Friday, I would do the same, and on Saturday, Allen would give the final "master's" reading. I knew Ginsberg's work quite well. I had read "Howl" as a teenager. I had even taught that poem, as well as the more accessible "America" as part of my junior English class offerings in American Lit.

Ginsberg is an icon to my students, but to me in those days he was someone more human and complex: a fellow war protestor whose courage I admired, a beatnik who heralded my own hippie youth, a notorious homosexual known for his forwardness. It was hard to separate the public figure from the artist. I knew that he had become part of the canon, but he was neither my favorite poet nor someone with whom I associated literary depth. He was a writer of the rant, the barbaric yawp of Whitman; one who shocked the establishment and etched a place for himself on the mutable wall of contemporary fame.

What a surprise then to attend his class on the French surrealists and watch writers, graduate students and professors struggling frantically to keep up with their notes as Ginsberg analyzed text, quoted lines from the poets in French, made biographical references, and connected literature to art and history. Eyes blazing above a trimmed beard, he was the epitome of a brilliant professor; not a sign of the ageing beatnik to be seen. His thick lips pursed as he thought of examples to illustrate his points; his New York accent was crisp and his delivery rapid. The lecture was a *tour de force*.

That evening the three of us were invited to conduct a discussion in the round which was televised by a local PBS affiliate. We answered students' questions on the art of writing, problems with revision, the importance of close reading in literature, and the value of the masters as models. At one point Diane Wakowski was holding forth on the feminine mystique in literature and I noted several of the students had begun to get that glazed look in their eyes which usually signals something less than rapt attention.

"Perhaps you should change the subject," I whispered to Allen. "I think we're losing some of our audience."

"Why don't you change the subject?" Allen replied.

"Because you have so much more authority," I said.

NEWPORT: A WRITER'S BEGINNINGS

"Just do it, Hogan!" Allen snapped. "Show some chutzpah."

I cleared my throat and then suggested that maybe we had belabored this topic long enough. "Perhaps we could turn to an earlier question, as to how a carefully chosen particular can suggest the universal?"

Allen smiled, then turned and kissed me right on the lips. "*Mazel tov!*" he crowed.

Just then the camera, which had been focused on Diane, suddenly shifted and presented the audience with the luridly thick lips of Allen connecting with my own.

Whatever the average viewer thought (or did not think) about my sexuality in those days, there was no question that my young wife of six months, who was watching the show at home, suddenly had reason for concern about my road trips. Nor was the fact that I was blushing madly as a sixteen-year-old lost on the students who sat around in the circle until one mercifully rescued me with a reply to the suggested topic change. Diane smiled knowingly, as if to say: *I am amazed at nothing men do.*

That evening Diane read from her recent book entitled *The Motorcycle Betrayal Poems* which she dedicated "to all the men who have ever betrayed me, in the hope that they will fall off their motorcycles and break their necks." It was a responsive audience, made even more so by the claque of young female groupies who sat in the front row and chuckled at her quips, applauded every poem, and added "Oh, wow!" in breathless whispers after every other verse.

The following evening I read my poems to a group which, although more subdued and not as emotive, was no less attentive. Like Diane, I managed to sell sufficient copies of my book to insure that next month's rent was covered. Allen, in his generous-spirited way, supported both our readings, and even stood in line until everyone else had gone before he stepped forward with his copy of my latest book to be autographed. Both Diane and I were touched by that.

Towards the close of the book signing, when we were drinking wine and eating strawberry crepes, the moderator suggested that those who wished to attend the Saturday Ginsberg reading sign up now. He said that the administration was concerned about seating and wanted to make sure there were sufficient chairs in the library, so that the reading would not be interrupted by shuffling and scraping. He also said that he expected some local citizens might be attending and so would place the sign-up sheet on the library desk where it would be available throughout the following day.

As we came out of the library into the muggy Pennsylvania dark, a dozen or more busses began arriving and parking in the lot below. When they discharged their passengers, the atmosphere of the campus changed at once. Young girls wearing shorts, tee-shirts and tennis shoes descended onto the tarmac and began singing scraps of songs, calling out to one another, collecting baggage and backpacks and heading to the dorms.

"They can't all be writers and editors," I remarked to Bill Welsh, aka "Grapey Welsh," a well-known and often misanthropic Pittsburgh poet.

"Nope. It's the Eastern High Schools Cheerleader Camp. Girls from all over New England came here to sharpen up their skills at cheering, tumbling, dancing. Probably not the most intellectual or cultured group of young ladies in attendance here."

"Oh, I don't know," I said. "Some cheerleaders these days are pretty sharp. Cheerleading is more like gymnastics, much more athletic than it was in the past."

"Still, I doubt many are interested in poetry..." he observed, as the raucous groups passed us in the parking lot, shouting and chanting as they headed for the empty dorms.

I didn't disagree.

The following day, Saturday afternoon, as we went about conducting our workshops and heard their voices raised on the athletic field, I pictured them, eluding their chaperones after lights out, descending on the town's little disco and bar, dancing up a storm and tempting the local boys, then coming home a little drunk and flushed after their night out. I envisioned at least one or two sick in the bathroom, getting caught by a wide-awake coach, and threatened with expulsion from the camp. The tears, the threatened phone calls to parents....

We went out for an early dinner on Saturday evening, and then returned shortly before Ginsberg's reading was scheduled to begin. When we got to the library at 7:30 PM we found that it was closed. A notice on the front door informed us that, due to the size of the crowd for the reading, it had been moved to the football stadium. What? It seemed incredible that Ginsberg could draw that large a crowd of townies from a little village in the Pennsylvania woods. This we had to see!

As we headed to the stadium we heard the din of the crowd. Not only were all the participants of the conference there and a couple of hundred folks from the town, but the entire contingent of cheerleaders as well. The open-air venue was packed with blow-dried and lipsticked blonds, chatting away as if this was just another event in their cheerleading agenda. Incredible! And what would the ageing beatnik/intellectual professor have to offer this motley crew? They seemed worlds apart.

As he strode to the stage in his dashiki and knitted yarmulke, the crowd hushed, and then burst into warm applause. The girls joined in and accompanied their applause with cheers, an occasional whistle, giggles and woos. Woos? Hmm. This will be interesting.

He played a few notes from his harmonium and then began to speak about death, the loss of his mother, the Jewish prayer for the dead. Then he read his haunting and well-known "Kaddish." The girls were quiet and respectful, as typical an audience for a poetry reading as you'd see at any college venue. Ginsberg was subdued as well. He read only a handful of poems as the evening progressed, perhaps three more of his own, a couple by William Carlos Williams, a long passage from Whitman, each piece drawing us into his inner world while opening us up to a language that was both concrete and expansive. Mostly he talked about art, about life.

And then as the hour wore down, he switched tactics. He began speaking of music, of Indian mantras, of incantatory verse and the importance of parallelism and repetition, of sound and echoes and how all of these had a spiritual essence. He talked about William Blake, the mystic, artist and poet who could write disturbing lyrics like "Tyger, Tyger," as well as simple, often sentimental Christian verses such as "The Lamb" ("Little lamb who made thee?"). Then Ginsberg actually sang each of these poems accompanied by the harmonium: "TY-ger, TY-ger, BURN-ing BRIGHT, in the FOR-est of the NIGHT/WHAT

immortal HAND or EYE, could FRAME thy FEARful SYM-
atree."

The girls cheered this rendition of a poem that most of
us had read at one time or another, but never actually
heard sung. Ginsberg told the students that these poems
were from Blake's *Songs of Innocence and Experience* and
were all written to be sung. He also reminded us of the
words of the Chinese poet Li Po: "Make it new! Make it
new!" and said that is what poetry was all about. He told
them that, just as their rendition of cheers and
gymnastics "snatched beauty from the jaws of time," poets
also look for ways to praise life that are unique while at
the same time realizing that they stand on the shoulders
of all those who went before and who taught us how to
dance and sing. Even poetry readings like this one, he
said, honor those who have gone before, remind us that all
dance, all song is prayer, and that our time here is short.
Carpe diem.

But now the stadium, which sat deep in a hollowed-out
valley that abutted the rolling Pennsylvania hills, had
begun to darken. Evening was descending and the sun
blinked in and out among the trees which bordered the
field. Ginsberg had waited too long to recite his well-
known "Howl," a long poem which would leave him
reading in the dark. It was almost time to end it. So,
which one of his favorite poems would he choose? "Walt
Whitman in the Supermarket"? "America"?

Now the strumming began again. And this time it was
the seldom-anthologized Blake poem called the "Nurse's
Song" that relates a story of children playing in the fields
as darkness is descending. Told by their mother that the
children must be in before nightfall, the nurse calls them.

But the children, wanting to take advantage of the last dying rays of the sun, are reluctant. Finally, they persuade the nurse to let them play just a little longer. The song with its haunting refrain of childhood goes like this:

When the voices of children are heard on the green,
And laughing is heard on the hill,
My heart is at rest within my breast
And everything else is still.
"Then come home, my children, the sun is gone down,
And the dews of night arise;
Come, come, leave off play and let us away,
Till the morning appears in the skies."

"No, no, let us play, for it is yet day,
And we cannot go to sleep;
Besides, in the skies the little birds fly,
And the hills are covered with sheep."
"Well, well, go and play till the light fades away,
And then go home to bed."
The little ones leaped, and shouted, and laughed,
And all the hills echoéd.

Now the light was fading behind the trees, and the cheerleaders all stood up in the green-gold twilight as Ginsberg began the refrain a second time:

And all the hills echoéd, and all the hills echoed,
And the little ones leaped, and shouted and laughed,
And all the hills echoéd.

Now the light voices of hundreds of teenaged girls joined him in his deep-throated amplified chorus, and the valley was filled with the sound of them, and we all rose and our voices joined in harmony chanting the ancient refrain again and again until all the hills indeed echoéd in the soft Pennsylvania evening. Oh, if only you had been there, when we were kissed by Allen Ginsberg.

THE DEATH MASTER

OVER MY DESK ARE two photos of my father who died at the age of sixty-one. The first shows him a fairly vigorous man of sixty, dressed in slacks, and in a white shirt with the sleeves rolled up on his muscled forearms. He is standing by a horse paddock on a farm in County Kerry. With him is my cousin John, a husky lad in his late twenties. My father and John are smiling comfortably, relaxed, and enjoying themselves. My father has a cigarette in his hand.

The second photo shows my father much debilitated and emaciated, dressed in a blue sports jacket, white shirt, and perfectly knotted scotch-plaid tie. He is seated on a piano stool with the piano behind him in the Victorian parlor of my grandparents' house. There was someone sitting next to him but that person has been neatly scissored out of the photo. My father's smile is tentative and not natural. Though not quite a grimace, it nevertheless speaks of pain and acceptance. His eyes are red-rimmed and watery. He is obviously sick. The photo was taken a month before his death of lung cancer which, according to my mother, was both unexpected and sudden.

My sister sent me these photos shortly after my father died. When I called my mother to talk to her about them, she expressed surprise that I thought my father looked terminal in the second picture. "I just thought he had a touch of the flu," she said. "He never complained. Even when he finally decided that he should go to the hospital, it was just a bit of a cough, but when they opened him up the cancer had spread throughout his insides. It was too late." When I asked her who cut her out of the photo, she again expressed surprise. "Oh, I remember being in that photo. But, no, I don't remember cutting myself out of it. Why would I?"

Why, indeed? Unless she felt that death was stalking her and, having already captured one half of the image might move on to the other half. My sister assures me that the picture came to her from my mother in that condition and no one else would have had the opportunity or inclination to cut her image out. But in all these years since my father's death, thirty-four to be exact, no explanation or even admission has ever been forthcoming from my mother. It's as if she edited her history along with my father's to reflect her absence from the day death first began its reconnaissance and then invasion of my father's body. There is a kind of Irish peasant wisdom in her which, despite her formal Catholicism, her middle class status, has never been eliminated. Perhaps, like the Ogallala Sioux in the 19th century who feared you would capture their spirit if you took their photograph, my mother was superstitious of leaving behind evidence that she accompanied the condemned is his final days.

When my father died in 1974, she was only fifty-nine which is still young in this century where fifty is the thirty of the previous generation. She was slim, did not smoke or drink, enjoyed walking, house cleaning, even doing laundry. She had no dishwasher in the kitchen, no microwave, no clothes drier in the basement. She did everything the old fashioned way, and hung up the clothes to dry on the line: two ropes stretched between wooden poles in the back yard. She did this even in winter, when the sheets froze and crackled in the December wind, while her knuckles reddened and cracked as she gathered the sheets like frozen sails in her chapped hands.

So much of what I know of her comes from the vivid years of my childhood living on Aquidneck Island, buffeted by winter storms, and seduced by summer visitors to Newport who had more money and more opportunities than those of us who served them could ever expect. Still, Newport was a beautiful town nestled among the elms and sycamores with the lavish mansions of the Gilded Age guarding the Ocean Drive. But even the loveliest of islands becomes stifling when you reach maturity and find that opportunities are rare, and social status is as real and more limiting than race. So, I left home when I was eighteen and never—well, almost never—looked back. I moved to another country finding both my hometown and the States too rigid, a plutocracy in which class (which was never discussed) was the only thing that really made a difference.

My mother was first generation Irish and raised in an immigrant family. She grew up during the Great Depression and married just before the war began. Rationing and penury were part of her upbringing and her idea of husbandry. A good wife was careful with budgets, bought nothing on credit, paid each bill as soon as it arrived, and saved every penny. This is why at ninety-two, she now has a house worth half a million, and another half a million in savings and investments. Despite this comfortable cushion, however, she continues to save scraps of soap, washes clothes by hand, and eats like a bird, making a can of tuna and a pack of saltines last for two days of lunches.

My sister who lives a couple of miles away brings her a hot meal each evening, makes sure her clothes are mended, and buys her pharmaceuticals and sundries. My brother-in-law mows the lawn, cuts the hedges and does minor repairs on the house. Of her wealth she says that she will leave everything to the Church because her children are both undeserving and ungrateful. While both these adjectives easily apply to me, my sister on the other hand has sacrificed years of her life, tending to her needs, doing her shopping and banking, taking her to doctors' appointments, dental appointments, to weddings and funerals. And, as I mentioned, bringing her a hot dinner and company each evening.

She is ninety-two and expects to live until she is at least one hundred and twenty, and we know this because when my bother-in-law calculated how long her money would last even if she were to double her current rate of expenditure (thirty years!), she said that was just about right, but she was still concerned that she would outlast her savings. There you have it in a nutshell, although what you have is not quite certain.

So, what does she do with her days? we wonder. She never leaves the house except when my sister takes her shopping or to the bank or a doctor's appointment. She uses an aluminum walker, does some small housework, watches TV, and reads the *Sunday (Catholic) Visitor* and the *Newport Daily News*. She is not, however, waiting for death. She expects to outlive everyone she has ever known, with a kind of mild defiance and delight. She is a survivor.

She knows that death is waiting all right. It is waiting for the neighbor kid who gets behind the wheel with no seat belt and a six pack of beer. It is waiting for the ruddy-faced executive who loads up on carbs and smokes his after-dinner cigar. It is waiting for the boys from West Virginia and Tennessee going off to fight in Iraq. And it is waiting impatiently for the last of her contemporaries including her ninety-four-year-old sister and her eighty-six-year-old neighbor. They, too, will grow weary of the New England winters, and fade into non-existence as all her friends and neighbors have over the years. Part of her *raison d'être* could very well be to see death take everything and everybody and leave her behind as a sole witness. She is a survivor.

Victor Frankl once wrote, "People can survive any *what*, as long as they have a *why*." He survived the Nazi prison camps because he created a reason to live, even as others perished daily in the brutal winters of Buchenwald. My mother is a true existentialist in this sense. She has focused on one enemy who has many allies, and she intends to stare him down.

"Of all the wonders that I have yet heard, it seems to me most strange that men should fear, seeing that death, a necessary end, will come when it will come." Unlike Caesar, however, death will not catch my mother unawares; she does not fear death but at the same time knows who death's friends and allies are, and will not let them into the house of her consciousness. She refuses to admit any thought, idea or suggestion that implies weakness, decrepitude, even normal ageing. She refuses to allow her grandchildren to call her "Grandma." She will shut off any conversations relating to her own condition, although she relishes hearing about the infirmities, illnesses and mortality of others, especially those younger than she. My sister's chronic pulmonary obstructive disease she sees as the wages of sin paid by an ex-smoker. The maiming and killing by roadside bombs of young boys in Iraq, she sees as a product of feckless poverty which put them in the army instead of at a good college. The cancers, heart attacks and strokes of neighbors in their seventies and eighties, she notes as a result of a weaker gene pool. She is a survivor, and each death she reads about in the obituary page is further proof that she is destined to continue, to outlast death, until death itself is but another neighbor gasping in his oxygen mask as she hobbles past him down the lane.

It is a narrow world, this austere life she has accommodated herself to in her island retreat. But to her there are no real options. I am reminded of a line from *Hamlet* where the young prince is told by Horacio that perhaps the isle of Denmark was too small for his ambitions, replies: "I could be bounded in a nutshell and count myself king of infinite space...." This is my mother in her room in the house my father built, alone and defiant, mistress of infinite space.

I look at the photo of my father again. His hands are crossed, his wedding ring conspicuously absent (his fingers had grown so thin that it would not stay on). His eyes are watery and strained, yet there is that forced smile of someone who is already seeing the other side and not liking much what he sees. He is three years younger than I in the photo and will not live another month.

There is a story that the Paul Auster character tells in the movie *Smoke* of a man who goes skiing in the Alps and is killed by an avalanche. Twenty-five years later his son climbs the same mountain to the peak. Then, halfway down, while he is resting and eating a cheese sandwich, he discovers the body of his father frozen in the ice. He looks down at him and has the strangest feeling that it is *himself* looking back at him. Even stranger is that fact that the self he is looking down at, is younger than he is right now. The boy has grown up and become a man, a man who is older than the father who died all those years ago.

That is how I am now looking at this photo of my father. And the fact that my mother has cut out her half of the photo, so that my father is alone on the piano stool, creates in my mind the illusion that anybody could have been there: my sister, my mother, my son, even me. With his perfectly-knotted Windsor, his crossed legs and tentative smile, my father watches us all grow old from his perch in the Victorian parlor. And, at this moment, I feel a bewildered and reluctant affinity for my mother in her single-minded defiance. When every force in the universe, including gravity, combines its energies to put you into the grave, the very fact of survival is the ultimate act of affirmation. There is nothing left to prove to anybody, only yourself; to know that you will be true in the end—not to the image of youth, nor to the social self of ambition and accomplishments, not even to the transcendent soul if it truly exists. You will simply be true to the brittle bones and translucent skin, the faded blue eyes and relentless brain which witness and hold in place one flickering flame against the dark.

IF YOU WERE THE ONLY GIRL IN THE WORLD

THE TWO SONGS I remember from my childhood were an Irish lullaby sung to me by my father as he walked the floors at night trying to get me to sleep, and "When She Wore a Tulip" which my uncle sang when I was a year and a half old. My mother considered it unremarkable that I had a clear memory of the Lullaby (Too-ra-loo-ra-loo-ra) because my father sang it even as I grew older. But she found it amazing that I remembered the other song which was sung by my Uncle Harry only once in my presence: the day he went off to war. Harry was dynamic, loud and extroverted, full of the gift of life and good cheer. On his last day at home, after a few beers, he had tossed me in the air, and told me that he would be home again before my second birthday. My protective mother watched in dismay as I went sailing in the air, and was happy and relieved, she told me many years later, when he was finally out the door and on his way overseas.

"When she wore a tulip a big yellow tulip and I wore a big red rose. When she caressed me, I knew that she loved me down where the blue grass grows," I would sing to myself in the days and weeks he was gone. It was December 1944 and Harry would not return from the Battle of the Bulge. He was killed by German artillery which smashed the trees in the forest where his platoon had dug in, sending deadly splinters and heavy trunks crashing down on him and his men. Two months later we received the telegram that he was killed in action. My mother's grief was re-doubled by her guilt.

As I grew older and helped around the house, I often listened to my mother sing as she washed dishes and I dried them while my sister cleared the table and swept up. My mother would sing "Dance with Me Henry," "The Yellow Rose of Texas," "Tennessee Waltz," "Are You Lonesome Tonight?" And "Who's Sorry Now?" But the sweetest song of all, which she sang in her pitch-perfect voice, went like this:

There would be such wonderful things to do
I would say such wonderful things to you
A Garden of Eden just meant for two
With nothing to bother you
If you were the only boy in the world
And I was the only girl.

I can't recall when we stopped singing together. I don't think we ever did. When I was in the glee club we would practice the song book together as I would rehearse in our basement for concerts. At parties we would sing Irish songs together. Even when she was in her eighties we sang "Danny Boy" and the "Rose of Tralee" in unison.

I remember her sitting on the back stairs that led to the basement listening to me practice my speeches for debate or public speaking competitions as well. She was a woman in love with music and language as much as she was in love with her son. But she was Irish and was of a generation where hugs and other tokens of affection were not in general usage. So we seldom shared anything personal except in a slanted way though poetry or song. She was also from an era when few women had a career outside the house so I also knew little about her hopes and dreams for her own talent. I suspect she sublimated them in raising her children.

I am thinking now how little I knew about her inner life and how much of a work in progress I was for her own creativity. How she gave me so many gifts: songs, ideas, scraps of poems, Irish history, a passion for language, impatience with pomposity, and with no idea whether any of it would amount to anything. Without knowing.

OLD SONG

She didn't know, couldn't have
my mother
that the singing as we washed dishes
in darkening New England nights
was part of all I am or will be.
The words she sang, sing now.

Those windows looked out on
a world cold and fierce.
Trouble was out there
the frost told me.
I'd find it soon enough.
But now belly filled
with boiled meat and cabbage
in her song I was
the only boy in the world
with nothing to bother you.

The man I became in the world
(her only boy still and forever)
had to do what he had to do.

Oh there are some who cling
to mothers the rest of their lives
mothers who do the same.
We were none of these.
Step by step we went our separate ways
her boy in the world prowling
the drunken dark cities
herself holed-up in damp Rhode Island rooms
as condos inched along side
and the last of the elm trees died.

First tree of my childhood. Young
mother. Youngest son.
Both too proud for rescue.
And distances geographic and fine
we never closed.
Never found a comfortable way either
to abandon ourselves
to passionate strangers.
We sheltered feelings
the only way we could:
words squirreled against the night.

Mother what I need to say
these days I can.
Life has made some fairly intricate moves.
I've gone beyond those childhood trees
and say this with the weight of years:
Your favorite line in the song is true.
The only girl in the world
was you.

EVERYTHING IN THE WORLD IS WAITING

IT'S SUNDAY MORNING AGAIN and I'm sitting in my garden beneath the mango tree watching a crow peck at scraps of desiccated wood in the high branches. My mother died on November 28 in her 93rd year. I said that I was watching a crow but that is only an educated guess. The bird is well-concealed by the leaves. I only assume it's a crow by the busyness and bluster. That (and a glimpse of a black wing with green highlights which is all I see) is sufficient for me to infer the entire shape. Later, other clues, his raucous caw as his leaps off the branches, his shadow against the whitewash of the garden walls, the distinctive shovel-shape of the tail, will flesh out his complete aspect.

Most of what we "know," most of what we do, is like that. We proceed through our lives with only bits and pieces of evidence and act on those bits and pieces as if the shape was whole and not a fragmented vision. Sometimes, it is enough. Other times we want more, as when we shape a narrative, or decide to shape our lives.

I wonder, though, if our narratives (this one, for example) like our complete lives aren't already there: inchoate, embryonic, waiting for us to unearth them. I'm reminded of a certain sculpture by Rodin which seemed to me unfinished when I saw it, in which a figure is seen emerging from the rock, one part recognizably human, the other stone-bound, trapped, never to come to life. I wondered if the artist died before he finished, or if he left the sculpture that way on purpose, to show the organic form emerging from the inorganic via his creative powers as a sculptor. More significant, though, is the fact that Rodin was able to "see" the form in the rock when it was— to the ordinary eye—simply rock, and was able to visualize clearly the human figure inchoate in the stone.

Michelangelo once ordered a slab of pure white marble wherein he had seen the exquisite form of young David, and he coaxed the young adolescent to emerge curve by curve from the unforgiving fastness of the crystalline limestone. Yet, one wrong move with the chisel and the face would be fractured. One chip too many and the delicacy of the hand would be lost.

And how did the sculptor begin, knowing that each cut of the chisel would determine forever and inexorably those which followed? How terrifying that pristine block of marble must have seemed. Did he invoke a Muse? Did he cautiously break off a piece here and there at the edge and test the consistency of the stone? Or did he confidently move to release what he knew was the young Israelite hidden in the stone, incipient, ready to be born in a more vividly sensual presence than had ever been pictured in scripture or imagination?

My guess is that there was nothing tentative about the first cut. The sculptor saw exactly that unique David concealed within the virgin marble. It may have taken days, even weeks before the vision coalesced, before he caught the curves and shadows, the fine veins and smooth musculature. But once he did, he moved confidently and without second thoughts. There was no room for second thoughts. Or regrets. No space for erasures, no super glue for wrong cuts or nicks. The making of the piece had both an innovative excitement for the artist and a finality.

Once he began, there was no stopping. David occupied all of Michelangelo's waking and sleeping hours. Under his fingers the body emerged in all its youthful exuberance, all its pubescent physicality. He lost all sense of hunger or thirst or weariness. He forgot his mother, his family, the pain in his wrist, the tendinitis in his shoulder. He forgot his past successes and failures. He forgot the smell of paint and canvas, the dust of rock and the marble chips. He forgot he was Michelangelo or that he was even an artist. He grew aware of the rhythm of the chisel and the vibrations in his fingertips and along his forearms. Then he forgot these sensations as well. His hair became tangled and sweat dripped into his eyes. He looked at the sculpture sometimes with longing and sometimes with fear. Then, after two days he went to bed.

He dreamed that he made a wrong cut and the front curls of David's hair were ruined and he had to remake him with a receding hairline. He dreamed that a muscle spasm caused an awkward tap with the hammer and David's penis was cut off. He awoke sweating, unable to eat, shivering with fever. He splashed his face with cold water. He picked up the chisel and felt himself trembling. He could not go on. He ate a chunk of stale bread and a piece of cheese. He drank a glass of wine. He told himself. "You were born to do this. This is your function. God has made you the instrument to release this handsome young man trapped in the inanimate whiteness. "

He fell to his knees and wrapped his hands around the inchoate figure, the unfeeling polished limestone, half chaos, half form. What if David refused to come out? What

179

if Michelangelo himself was not worthy? He knew that reputation did not make the artist. What he had done prior to this had no meaning and no substance. This David, this statue, this act of creation was the only thing that mattered. If he failed here he would fail everywhere, no matter what the critics might say, no matter what history might say. He would fail for all time.

He picked up the chisel. At least the shaking had gone away. And he told himself that the spirit had not brought him this far to fail. He knew that true genius consisted in something ordinary people never guessed at: obdurate persistence. He began again to chip away at the unforgiving marble. He came this time to it with no expectations, with total humility, with the belief that David was a gift which he was merely unwrapping a chip at a. time. And what happened then was amazing. The marble flaked off gently as soapstone. The muscles of David's biceps were smooth and rounded on the first cut without any effort to mold them. That which was awkward, rough, serrated, fell away, and the stone surface became lubricous, the thigh muscles like satin, the cheek silken. It was impossible to cut the wrong way, the veins rolled out like serpents along the delicate line of the forearm. Everything flowed as if molded from white lava: the glossy pectorals, the sleek abdominals, the unwrinkled, glossy sex.

As Michelangelo worked, a David appeared which had never been seen before, never imagined. And as he worked his hammer and chisel, mere tools to his vision, and himself a tool for the spirit, the spirit became flesh, or the closest a sculpture can come to flesh. A shining, perfect creature was born, a pagan *inamorato*, half Eros, half

Dionysius, whose very stillness seemed to imply motion and whose youth belied antiquity.

The head and the torso were done. What remained were the thighs, the knees, the calves, the feet, an occasional refinement of the eyes. This time when Michelangelo went to sleep he had no dreams. He woke the next morning refreshed to the sound of doves cooing under his window, and the shouts of young girls playing in the street.

David's legs were tensed as he leaned, not with a sling casting a rock at Goliath, nor even to escape from the rock that imprisoned him, but rather learning towards the children playing in the streets below that Michelangelo heard beneath his window that final morning. And the lips were parted, not in an effort to kill the giant, but in pleasant anticipation of a day in the Italian countryside drinking chilled wine and resting beneath the ancient olive trees far from his Semite home.

Yet this is not about Michelangelo or David, but about the gift of seeing the figure in the stone, seeing the narrative in the blank page, seeing your life pure and whole, as you chip away at the encrustations of the years.

William Stafford describes a moment which, until I had read his poem, I would have thought to be ineffable. He wrote:

Thus freedom always came nibbling at my thought,
just as—often, in light, on the open hills—
you can pass an antelope and not know
and look back and then--even before you see—
there is something wrong about the grass.
And then you see.

That's the way everything in the world is waiting.

Stafford shared a narrative which went along with this poem. He said that when he was a young boy about ten or eleven, his father and he were tramping in the woods looking for game. His father said, "Keep a sharp eye peeled, Bill. You can see things better than I can."

Stafford was delighted. His father, a veteran woodsman, had told the young Stafford that the boy had superior vision. Or perhaps he meant closer powers of observation. What a gift! It gave the youthful Stafford permission to be a see-er, an observer, one with a gift which was superior to even that of his father.

Later, when he had become older, Stafford realized that perhaps all his father meant was that his own eyes were failing with age. But that was unimportant. The emotional and spiritual effect on the young ten-year-old had a lifelong impact. Stafford assumed the mantle of careful observer or seer, of a visionary with all the existential power this could carry for him as a poet. His father, whether inadvertently or not, had given him permission to speak, permission to report to generations to come his unique vision of the world.

To me that is such a powerful moment. What makes it so powerful is the boy's recognition of its importance, or at least his assigning it importance. And it makes no difference what the father's intent was. For whether the moment was a teaching one or the son's interpretation was value-added, the result was the same. That moment freed the young boy to see clearly and uniquely what previously had been seen and talked about only by others.

As a teacher, I am always in search of a path I can offer my students to realize their own visions, while at the same time keeping my own vision as a writer unclouded by hours of correcting their essays and exams. This appears to be one such path. Equally important, it offers a way of living which is dynamic, authentic and self-actualizing, while at the same time encouraging humility because after all, David, the young Israelite; the antelope on the hill, and even one's own life, were there all the time. All the artist and the poet did, all any of us do at our very best, is discover what has been given to us to find. Then with patience, close attention and discipline, carefully trace the lines.

And mothers help more than sons ever guess at, and even their graves in the rain.

For Anna F. Hogan (1913-2008), in loving memory.

WORKS BY MICHAEL HOGAN

POETRY

Letters for My Son (1975)
If You Ever Get There, Think of Me (1976)
Soon It Will Be Morning (1976)
April, 1976 (1977)
Rust (1977)
Risky Business (1978)
The Broken Face of Summer (1981)
Making Our Own Rules (1989)
Imperfect Geographies (1998)
Winter Solstice: Selected Poems 1975-2012

FICTION

A Lion At A Cocktail Party (1978)
Molly Malone and the San Patricios (1998)
A Death in Newport (2011)
Molly Malone y Los San Patricios. Trans. by Ivy Becerra. (2012)

NON-FICTION

Intelligent Mistakes: Grammar Supplement for Latin Americans Writing in English (1991)
The Irish Soldiers of Mexico: A History of the San Patricio Battalion (1997)
Los Soldados Irlandeses de México. Trans. by Clever Chávez Marín. (1998)

A Writers Manual for Inmates in Correctional Institutions (2001)

Teaching from the Heart: Working At International Schools in Latin America (2003)

Savage Capitalism: Latin America in the Third Millennium (2010)

Newport: A Writer's Beginnings (2012)

MICHAEL HOGAN is the author of twenty books, including *The Irish Soldiers of Mexico*, which was the basis for an MGM film starring Tom Berenger and an award-winning documentary on the St. Patrick's Battalion. His writing has appeared in *the Paris Review, The Harvard Review*, the *Bloomsbury Review, the American Poetry Review* and dozens of textbooks and anthologies. His book *Winter Solstice: Selected Poems 1975-2012* has been praised by Sam Hamill for writing that "bears the weight of hard-earned experience together with the sweet light of an open and generous heart." Hogan is the recipient of the National Endowment for the Arts Fellowship, the Alden Dow Creativity Fellowship and the Colorado Humanities Fellowship. He lives in Guadalajara, Mexico, with the textile artist Lucinda Mayo and their dog Molly Malone.

www.drmichaelhogan.com